LIVE YOUR DREAM IN 7Ds

Achieving The Life You Desire, One Step At a Time!

Otieno Paul-Peter, Esq

Foreword by

Larry Liza

Dissecting The Secret!

Publisher's note:

Live Your Dream Enterprises Ltd
P.O Box 101748-00101 Nairobi, Kenya.
www.liveyourdream.co.ke

Ordering Information:
Quantity sales. Special discounts are available on quantity purchases by corporations, associations, and others. For details, contact the publisher at the address above.

First Printing, 2017

ISBN 978-9966-103-15-4

TABLE OF CONTENT

Foreword

The world has an overflow of books on personal development yet many still languish in the soggy soil of unexploited potential. Authors have availed broths of knowledge for humanity, yet only a few of us rise to drink from these pots. All of us who choose to drink react differently, possibly from the packaging of the materials or simply, their personality. And so, all end as the seeds of the parable that responded differently based on the ground upon which they fell.

I have finally laid my hands on a book that is a fertile ground for all and sundry, irrespective of race or gender, region or religion, for we all desire to reach the stars and live our dream. *Live Your Dream in 7Ds* shares common principles packaged in an 'out of the world' yet simplistic manner.

Here is a chance to dream as is the reality of life that goes beyond the famed 3D. Once you *Dream*, curve your niche and walk and work through it, with *Determination* as a key armour of your heart, rising when fallen and trudging on. Discover the place of *Discipline* in helping you focus with every step you make and every breath you take. See the reality of the days of our lives, though *Disappointments* always come our way, to stay rooted and established in the soil of our faith. For once I see that to *Detour* is never necessarily negative, but we can stick to our goal, inspiration, vision and stay true to our emotions. The call to *Detox* is the crown jewel of this, outlining principles for our renewal. And to crown it all, to *Dream Again,* on and on, to live and let live, and achieve the potential God created us for, our very purpose for life. Live Your Dream!

Larry Liza

Director, World Customs organization, East & Southern Africa. Larry is also a Performing artist (Poet) and a Global Champion for White Ribbon Alliance.

Preface

Having grown up in an economically deprived family, where no meal was guaranteed and basic needs were scarcely met, where the only care was just to survive the day and nothing more, I kept having a feeling that life could not really be that unfair. That a so loving GOD could not have intended for some people to live a life of perpetual suffering while others swim in wealth and bliss. In my mind, I believed there was something wrong that needed to be made right. I wanted to know why some people could, seemingly, be living in abundance while others have to be content with empty stomach. Why some struggled greatly to be in school while others seemed to have all the money for the fees, holidays and more. Why some of the people who seemed bright and reasonable were also poor and unfulfilled and yet others who seemed blunt academically were doing much better in life.

My curiosity and passion led me to study everything I could and seek from everywhere possible that I may find answers to these and some other difficult life puzzles. I was determined to find satisfactory explanations, if they exist, and share the information, if only to let people be contented or to enlighten them to achieve the so called success in life. Well, it has been over three decades and here , in this book, is what I have to show. I am so proud of this that, even if I will have nothing else to bequeath my children, this book is good enough to guide them to be what they want to be and, perhaps, better than all that the schools will provide them.

Originally, my intention was to simply teach these life principles to individuals, more so family members, through one-on-one discussions and in small family gatherings, plus a few friends. I did not have an idea about writing a book; let alone the notion that there could be such like books already in existence. After all, who would have wanted to read my book and why! Just a poor boy from a tiny village in a third-world country somewhere in Africa, I could not have thought of that! In our clan, no one wanted to listen to our family! We were among the poorest of the poor; with lots of problems including diseases and less education, limited exposure..name it! Besides, my dad was extremely alcoholic and the least likely to be asked for any advise. We had no proper shelter, with grass-thatched, leaking roof over our heads such that no one would sleep the moment it starts to rain. We used plastic cups to fetch the rain-water from the leaking roof; trying to ward it off from wetting our torn, reed marts and sisal sacks which served as our beds. That was the story then, looking back, now I say how things can change when we choose to change; to pursue our dreams with unwavering focus and determination!

Today, after deeply pondering and contemplating my life purpose, having gone through it all and experienced what is both necessarily and sufficient, I have chosen to share my real life experience through this short book, and the lessons gathered alongside, with the intention that this may be able to help someone else get to Live the life he or she so much desires. If a life can improve, even by 10%, after reading this book, it will have achieved its purpose!

In putting together these real life stories and instructions, I have, as much as possible, kept the language simple enough and the ideas so practical that virtually everyone who shall read this book will not need extra effort to understand and apply the lessons. It is a book for anyone with a dream. It is a book to help people live a more fulfilling and meaningful life. In my view, this book could be one of the simplest, most elaborate and complete version in this field of Living Your Dream. It shall definitely touch the lives of millions allover the world. Read it and digest it. If you happen to like it, I'll be happy to get your feedback. I might just include your feedback in the next review. Stay blessed. Live Your Dream! Enjoy.

Otieno Paul-Peter,
pp@liveyourdream.co.ke

Reviews

As a person who knows the writer so well, I can attest that Otieno Paul-Peter, indeed, is a symbol of courage, determination, hard work and unwavering focus. I personally witnessed some of the experiences Paul went through! This Book "YOUR DREAM IN 7Ds" is an exact walk through the life of the writer; it is not just a motivational book. It is a life transforming book which gives the reader an in-depth mind of "Living One's Dream". May the Lord God continue to bless you, my brother Paul.

Musa Obuba

Elder at CITAM Valley Road Church

Acknowledgement

First and foremost, I pass my sincere appreciation to my beloved family, including my loving wife, Edna and our lovely children, for their relentless support in this journey. Much gratitude and love to my great editor, Njeri Mwathe, for the wonderful and selfless effort in putting the language in acceptable form. To my friend Julius Mwangi who could not stop pushing me to put these thoughts in writing for posterity. My mentor, Maurice Makoloo, and all those of you who aided me in one way or the other for the successful production of this material, may God bless you all. I am deeply indebted to my long time friend, Larry Liza, for accepting to read, endorse and foreword this book for me. It is a great honor that comes with a lot of humility. Thank you all the leaders who have endorsed this message so far. Words cannot express the amount of joy and enthusiasm you people have put into my heart.

Equally noteworthy is the ceaseless effort of my cover designers, Digicreative Designs Technology Limited. Your work is excellent. Stay blessed.

Dedication

To all the people who have dreams and would like to live a more meaningful life. I also dedicate it to my beautiful daughter, Cecilia, who seats next to me every time I am writing and helps in various ways.

Chapter 1

DREAM, IT IS.

Why Do You Get What You Don't Want?

The reason you are presumably reading this book is to achieve a certain goal or dream. It may be one or you could be having a number of them. Congratulations! It is the first and major step. One of the strangest truths in life is that you cannot achieve what you do not know. You cannot get what you do not expect. I often say that only expectant mothers deliver. This is true in the visible as in the invisible realms of life. To expect is to get. On your journey to success, you must, first of all, get clear about what success really means to you. The key word here is 'CLEAR'. That is the starting point towards Living Your Dream! It means you must have that DREAM in the first place before you set out to achieve it. Else, you will achieve whatever may be clear in your mind. Whether it is your dream or nightmare. It is that simple! And didn't I warn you that it is going to be really simple? In case I didn't, now you know.

It is often amazing how simple the path to success can be and yet many people ignore it. Others postpone. We call it procrastination. Others take time to 'think about it'. I remember a speaker, one of my all time classic speakers, Jim Rohn, said in one of his talks; "*whatever is easy to do is also easy not to do.*" I agree. And that is why we see more people 'failing' to do them. They are simply failures. Failing to do is a failure. Easy to do, easy not to do. The choice, therefore, is yours; to do or not to.

> *As much as possible, ensure you are absolutely clear about what you want!*
>
> *---Otieno Paul-Peter---*

You may already know this, that, people often get things they do not want more often than they get those things they want, and they keep wondering why. There is no need to wonder why. Rather, wonder, why not! The reason I am saying this is that the formula for achieving that which you do not want is not any different from the one for achieving what you want; only that it is simpler. Nature has it that way! And most of the times it is the same old ignorance, that we tolerate, that causes us to keep getting the same results. Thank GOD that from today onwards, you are going to discover this great secret. Actually, it is not really a secret. It is a secret to those who had not discovered it. Ignorance is the greatest liability of mankind! You are now fighting it ruthless and, I can assure you, that your success is within reach! And in this (your) fight, I want to repeat, if you are really sure about where you are going, you have higher chances of getting there. You can even ask for direction along the way. Not very true for the opposite scenario. If you do not know where you are going, you can't get there! A way will always be created, if it does not already exist, but only to those who are clear about where they are going. You do not have to know how it is going to happen. Neither do you have to know the direction to where you want to go in order to start. It is not your part. Your work is to be crystal clear about where you want to go. The person you want to become, what you want your life to be. Be sure of the dream and 'make it clear'.

In the book of Habakkuk, in the bible, GOD tells the prophet to "*write his vision down and make it clear in order that whoever reads it may get it clearly*". In fact, in another version it says, 'so that whoever sees it may run'. What excites me is the word 'run'. It is the same stuff we are talking about; the capacity to understand it readily and get excited about it!

If only I know where I'm going-
Then no one will hold my loin.
For in my favor even the winds will blow
And to achieve it my ability will grow
So long as I know -
where I'm going!
----Otieno Paul-Peter---

> *Success, in many ways, is like a journey.*
>
> *---Brian Tracy---*

Success, in many ways, is like a journey. Whenever we set out to go to a particular destination, we are very clear and precise about every detail, including the time we expect to reach, the means of transport and everything else. We keep our focus on our destination no matter what happens along the way, and thus we more often than not, tend to reach where we had set out to go. That is the same way we achieve anything we want.

When I was in Form IV, final year in secondary school, preparing for my final exams that would qualify me for a degree course, through the talks and discussions with one of the tutors who was serving as an untrained teacher in our school because he was still in the university and studying something else not leading to education, I developed an interest in one of our higher learning public institutions. It was, and still is, the best and largest higher learning institution in our country. I was so enthusiastic about it that I kept saying to myself, *"Mimi naenda jiji"*..(I am going to the city) when talking about which university I would join. It was clear in my mind. In my form IV, it was obvious that I had to start the secondary school syllabus all over again because I was just rejoining school after over a year out of school, and did not have any book brought forward from my previous schooling. But still, I managed to qualify for the entry into the university and part of the reason is, I was clear about where I was headed.

In this book, you are going to get many examples. But the best example should come from you. Start evaluating yourself and everything that ever happened to you. Reflect back and start collecting your thoughts how it played in your mind before it happened and the feelings you had.

Believe me or not, this is something I have learnt with pain and awe. We tend to get what is inherent in our hearts. We always achieve what we know and are clear about; good or bad! Ever noticed that a great majority of people tend to get more of what they do not want than what they want? If not, start checking now. Start where you are. Start with yourself! Unless you are already successful; as successful as you would like to be, you most likely are experiencing this nightmare. Today, and in this chapter, I want to give you the very reason such funny things happen. It is the same reason we have more weeds than crops in the fields. The reason we have more diseases than drugs. This is the root-cause of all ills and all beauty.

The reason almost all personal growth coaches tell you to write goals is hinged on this principle. Not everyone may realize it, including the teachers themselves. But I thank GOD for this revelation. I kept looking till I got it. Your mind is the center of your whole being. **Whatever happens in your life on the outside, has a direct relationship with**

what happens in your life from within. This is a fundamental truth and indisputable! I am a scientist and I have come to appreciate it.

If you have to remember one thing from this book, remember the statement highlighted above and instill it in your mind. Read the statement as many times as will be necessary for you to understand it absolutely. Because therein lies everything upon which our discussion shall proceed. What it means is, till now, you have been creating your life as you go along. You are the author of the exact life situations and circumstances you find yourself involved in. If I am the first to break this news to you, I am very sorry if it offends you but very happy if it makes you happy and empowers you. Either way, it is the truth and, as you probably already know, it is the TRUTH that sets you FREE. Nothing else! Notice that my purpose is to assist you to be FREE in order that you may Live Your Dream! That you may succeed.

> *Our inner world creates our outer world.*
>
> *---T. Harv Eker---*

When I had done my Kenya Certificate of Primary Education (KCPE) examinations, I knew that I was going to pass. That was not the problem. I knew I would get a calling letter to a good school, that was not a problem either. But I was not clear about which school I wanted to go to. I was, instead, clear about which school I did not want to join. That was our village school where I had done most of my primary schooling; Kendu Muslim School. Guess what? I could not avoid going there! I got what I hated with passion, but what I was very clear about. If you check in your life, you most likely have a similar story. You either got the school you really wanted or the one you really resisted! Why? And how do I know this! It is because of the law of non-resistance! **What you resist persists!** In the bible, the scripture says 'resist not evil', and 'win evil by good'. This could be why.

And just like I was so clear about which university I wanted to be in and all the rest were therefore clouded and never given 'mental space', I got it. At this point, it is good to reiterate what an anonymous author once said, 'no thought resides in your mind rent-free'. It is true. I would be excited whenever I thought of the University of Nairobi and imagining myself part of that great institution. Actually, I can pinpoint almost everything in my life and how I attracted it. You too should be able to. I will relate to you more as we continue. For now, what you need to know is that you will always get what you are clear about. What is in your mind? What is your dream? What life do you want for yourself? Are you able to make it so clear in your mind that if you gave someone such an order to go bring it, if it were possible to do so, he/she would deliver it to you without a mistake? If so, you have covered the major part in Living

> *What you resist persists.*
>
> *---Law of Non-resistance---*

Your Dream! you are more likely to achieve it now.

Again, learn to get out of your mind what you do not want. Do not concentrate on them, do not imagine them, never give them 'mental space'. They will grow into reality. Your mind is a double-edged sword. It gives you what you do not want just as readily as what you want. You only need to know how to make good use of it. If you do not want to be married in Kabuoch, for example, stop talking about it, stop thinking about it. Just identify where you want to be married and concentrate your thoughts on that with power and imagination. And the more you apply this knowledge, the better you become at it and the more exciting life becomes. You should now be happy that you are taking control of your life and mastering your destiny, aren't you? Remember the law of use and disuse?

> *Whatever you do not use, you lose!*
>
> *---Law of use and disuse---*

It matters not how strait the gate,
How charged with punishments the scroll.
I am the master of my fate:
I am the captain of my soul.
---Invictus by William Earnest Henley--

Creating Something From Nothing

Everything you see around you was created, first in the mind, then in reality. Even GOD the Father of ALL creation started from nothing except the mind (which we call energy at another level). The first step in creating something from nothing, therefore, is in forming it in your mind and making it clear. If you want a house, first of all, make it clear in your mind what sort of house you want, how big, how you want the interior to look like, and all the details. Your mind will, thus, start going to work until it becomes a reality. Even getting a baby starts in the mind; either you strongly oppose it or strongly go for it. A job, a course, passing exams, anything.

> *Whatever we persistently hold in our minds, that we shall hold in our hands.*
>
> *---Otieno Paul-Peter---*

I once read a story online. It was an old lady who was asking a very renown pastor a question about what happened of her prayer and wish. The pastor would get a number of questions and choose one among them to publish and so it was this one that was published and being a subscriber, I got the same email. The lady asked: “I can't understand why I am in a nursing home while all the while I have been praying to God that I may not go to the nursing home! How come GOD did not answer my prayer?” Sorry to say, but the pastor did not even understand why and instead started explaining in the ordinary pastoral way...that God's ways are not our ways,..blah blah. But I believe I do understand it because the same GOD who created everything created these natural laws and it is not likely that He can contradict Himself. The lady had her mind filled with images of nursing home; what she didn't want.

I tell you the truth. This is the law. GOD cannot blatantly disobey His own laws that He had approved. If you can see it in your mind, you can seize it in reality! What would you have told the lady? She did not know how to convert something from nothing. Just like the universe was built from nothing. This point is just to emphasize the idea of getting clear about your goals and objectives. The greatest work is in the mind, not in the body. In the thinking realm, not in the doing realm. Doing is a consequence of thinking.

The universe conspires

A way shall be created to him who knows where he is going. Once you know what you want and have become very clear about it, you are now more likely to achieve it than ever. Even 'miraculously'. And mostly so! Why? Because you are starting to be in harmony with the greatest creative energy. The Universe of Power. You are starting to invoke your natural powers that make you a 'god', being the image and likeness of GOD the Father. This is where everything starts to work in your favor; to ensure you get that which you are working on. We shall discuss this in this book bit by bit. It is written in the scriptures; 'all things work together for the good of those who love GOD.' Seen in another way, the converse is most likely true. But what I want to emphasize is that once you are already mentally clear about your goals, your dreams, a way shall be created to aid you achieve it because every force in the universe start conspiring to work for your good or otherwise; depending on what is clear in your mind.

The Right Tools

You must, therefore, learn how to set goals. Goals being the first basic tools for working on your dreams. Goals, logically, become the seedlings for your dream. They help you to have an idea of what you want and to become as specific as possible; just like you are ordering for a phone from a dealer. You can't just say, “I want to buy a phone”. You must give details in order for the dealer to be able to picture what you actually want. In other words, if you think of your mind as a computer operating system, goals form a programming language for your mind. That is, using clearly defined goals, you will be able to give clear instructions to your mind about what you want. Lack of this knowledge has caused failure throughout history and counting.

> *The power that is within us is enormous. We only need but to learn how to use it.*
>
> *---Otieno Paul-Peter---*

Allow me to break this news to you. It may not be very good news but it is important to know. Ready? Here it is: **the only major reason majority of the people do not get what they really desire to have in life is because they do not really know what they desire!** I know that statement sounds mouthful and repetitive. But it is the truth. Many people you see around are clear about what they do not want, thus they keep getting them. You only get what you are crystal clear about.

One of the ways to be clear about what you want is to go shopping for it; have some images of the same and ensure you burn them into your mind by constantly concentrating on them and admiring them. If you do this with *ample degree of emotions*, if you can really feel it in your heart and see yourself (in your mind) having achieved that which you want, you will be surprised at the results. Time is not a factor here! Things can happen much faster than you even expect. When I was still dreaming about joining the University one day, it looked like it would take over a decade. Did it? Never! It was much earlier than I had ever imagined! Imagination is POWER!

> *Imagination is Power!*
> *---unknown---*

A story is told of a boy who was obsessed about becoming a pilot. This is a true story and it happened very recently, that is, after 2010 in Nairobi Kenya. This boy, though quite brilliant and scoring fantastic grades in his academics, seemed to have minimal chances of Living his Dream because his parents had average income at best. They were very certain about their inability to afford such an expensive course and thus feared they were going to be a great disappointment to their only son. No relative or friend could come to their aid, at least as far as they were concerned. For some reason, they had thought that such a 'fantasy' would come to an end along the way and their son would, perhaps, pick another discipline, may be one of those offered in public universities and that would be a great relief.

> *Whatever a man's mind can conceive and believe, that he can achieve.*
>
> *---W. Clement Stone---*

In their ingenuity, they chose to avoid that topic and, instead, talk well of other alternative disciplines, hoping that would influence the lad to change his mind. This, however, did not divert the focus of the boy. He kept looking at photos of airplanes and pilots, sticking the images plucked from newspapers and magazines on the wall of his tiny room, and browsing the Internet about planes. It was an obsession! It was a **Burning Desire**! The boy had a dream and was clear about it. The parents equally got pretty clear about what they did not want and resisted it with all passion, but not remembering to be clear about what they wanted of their son, other than a good life.

As the exams were nearing, the tension and anxiety

heightened. The parents were holding their breath, hoping he fails to meet the required aggregate and qualifies for other equally lucrative courses, the boy determined to excel well and get fully qualified for admission into his dream-course, aviation school. He had plans in place, knew what it would take and went for it. He paid the full price. Exams came and he sat for them.

You are right! He passed 'with flying colors' and amazed everyone! Time had come for him to make that next important step. His parents did not even know how to start suggesting other alternatives. Their tricks could not suffice anymore. They were filled with both fear and shame. They clearly could not see in their wildest dreams how they could afford to take their victorious boy to an aviation school.

The good news is, he went to such a school, a much better one off-course, abroad! It happened and today he is Living his Dream! How did it happen? Who paid it? Call it luck or whatever you will, but once as he was browsing the Internet in his usual obsession, just when time for college was beckoning, he came across a scholarship opportunity abroad, applied and qualified. What do you attribute that to? I leave it for you to decide. I know of countless other stories. But in general, remember:

1:What you resist persists
2:What you fear perseveres
3:To desire is to expect
4:How is non of your business.. it will happen!

You will be what you will to be;
Let failure find its false content
In that poor word, "environment,"
But spirit scorns it, and is free.

It masters time, it conquers space;
It cows that boastful trickster, Chance,
And bids the tyrant Circumstance
Uncrown, and fill a servant's place.

The human Will, that force unseen,
The offspring of a deathless Soul,
Can hew a way to any goal,
Though walls of granite intervene.

Be not impatient in delay,
But wait as one who understands;
When spirit rises and commands,
The gods are ready to obey

---- James Allen ----

Identifying Life's Purpose

Here is a topic that eludes many people. Some do not even want to think about it because it causes them some sort of mental torture. Have you ever posed to think of your purpose in life? Has it ever bothered you to know the reason you were created, in case you believe in the creation theory like I do?Here is another way to put it; what would you like to be remembered for?

Not long ago I was talking to a lecturer. He had been a great success in the field of finance in the public sector and had retired or so did I think. He went back to class to pursue his PHD while working as a lecturer. He had just read a story about me that appeared in one of the dailies. He was asking if I could speak to his son. As we kept talking, he said, "but you are lucky. You seem to have known about your calling early and started pursuing it. What would you say of someone like me at this age?" His voice sounded of despair. I learnt a great deal out of that conversation! Is there such a thing as the right time for us to know our purpose in life? And who is responsible?

Many people look for happiness but do not seem to find it. We keep thinking that 'if I get this degree, I'll be happy', 'if I get that job I'll be really happy' or 'if only I would get married (to so and so) I'd be very happy'.... But soon after that happens, you realize that the happiness you expected is either absent or short-lived. This is because we haven't attached a major value to our lives and thus keep living to either impress others or look for attention.

> *If you live without a life mission, you are as good as not living! Because you will not be happy!*
>
> *--Otieno Paul-Peter--*

One of the reasons you see or hear majority of people tired of their jobs is because they have no major value attached to it except to pay bills. Go around and ask people, one at a time, 'why do you work?' and you will quickly realize that people work just because they have to. No drive, no major mission. They do what they do because they do not have a choice. This brings lethargy and boredom. People just going through the movements. It is one of the greatest causes of despair and even harmful indulgences that cause troubles in families, workplaces, communities.

Have you ever heard of some people saying TGIF? _ Thank God It's Friday? Or those who say like, 'this day has really been long', 'this month is not coming to an end..'.? That tells you something; they are not enjoying what they do. They are not having fun! You cannot Live Your Dream in such circumstances.

A writer once said, “The two most important days in your life are the day you are born and the day you discover why you were born.” If up to this day you have never bothered about this, I urge you most solemnly, kindly do it. Do it now, do it immediately. Let this thought provoke your heart and pierce your soul. Immerse yourself into it and start thinking about it until you have an answer. I will try to give you a few guides and hints then you go do the homework. It will make you rejuvenate your life and get excited once more, if not all the more; perhaps for life. You will feel exhilarated and wanting to wake up and go do what you were meant to do. It is, ultimately, the start of living your dream. Living a life of bliss and fulfillment. Of all the people who are truly Living their Dreams, you will hardly find one who is doing what he/she doesn't believe is his/her life purpose.

> *The two most important days in your life are the day you are born and the day you discover why you were born*
>
> *---Unknown---*

All great leaders in history, all celebrities and stars, all heroes are whom they are because, somehow, they discovered their purpose and opted to pursue it, deliberately or otherwise. The Creator is a Supreme Being of diversity. He never meant that everyone should be the same, doing the same things. Take, for example, if a man creates or builds anything. Does he just do it aimlessly? Without purpose? Not really. When we make a vehicle, we know exactly what it is meant to do. We cannot put a tractor to be a Public Service Vehicle(PSV). We cannot use a car to plough. If we build a house, we know exactly what it is meant for and thus equip it appropriately. Isn't it, therefore, logical that the

Ultimate Creator had to have a sole purpose for every creature and thus fully equip them for the predetermined purpose? I think so. It cannot be otherwise!

If you join me in accepting the above stated reasoning, then you must also join me in this: You also have a purpose in life and as long as you are not pursuing this your preordained purpose, you are not likely to achieve any reasonable level of happiness and fulfillment. Imagine a cow put to yoke for plowing instead of an ox. Imagine Mike Tyson (Iron Mike) put to 100m race in the Olympics and not boxing. Imagine Mike Jordan in a football pitch. No way! Could that be you? Fully equipped and endowed for a certain field but trying luck in some other domain? I hope not. If you think otherwise, you are probably right.

At this point, it is necessary for us to agree that if you look at your natural talents and gifts , you probably are not far from what you could do best. List some of the things you are naturally good at; check your academics, your extra curricular activities, your heart, and your talents. If you group these things, you may be able to get a convergence. That should be able to point clearly what you were meant to be. The convergence between what you are good at doing and what you really love doing and draws natural enthusiasm from, enthusiasm that begets creativity and induces the extra-mile principle in you, the extra-mile principle lack of which success tends to elude many a people. It is never too late, in case you are in a different field and feeling pissed off, to re-live your purpose and re-kindle your dream! You can do it! We know of people who joined athletics in their 50s and won gold medals at 80s. Again it is never too early. You are not too young. No reason can block you. Whether disability, background, education,...whatever it may be. Nothing at all except you. I'm told of an African Proverb that says, '***if there is no enemy within, the enemy without can do you no harm.***'

> *If there's no enemy within, the enemy without can do you no harm.*
>
> *---African Proverb---*

It is not easy to become a big success in a field where you are not naturally or genetically biased to; I mean, in a field that is really foreign to your being. It may be difficult to believe or to conceptualize, but in order to illustrate this, imagine if Jesus Christ changed His life's mission from Salvation and Establishment of GOD'S kingdom to fishing and feeding people with Nutritious sea Delicacies or Building Low cost houses to house the less fortunate or to running a carpentry workshop. Perhaps very few would have noticed him and most likely not many people would still be talking about Him over 2000 years later. Do you agree? How about if Amadeus W. Mozart chose to pursue another discipline, say law, as opposed to music? And for your information, it is said the Bill Gates parents had wanted him to, and insisted that he should, go study law. What would have happened if he only bulged out of respect and followed the desires of his parents?

Another example is this, suppose Nelson Mandela chose to be a lecturer in a university, for example Oxford University, lecturing political science or if he ended up being, perhaps, a civil Engineer in South Africa, may be he would not have achieved nearly close to what he did in his political career. And that does not necessarily imply that such alternative paths are mean or of less importance. We have had others in such fields who became great too! But every leader rises to greatness because of choosing to defy the common beliefs or logical arguments and then daring to follow what the heart shows him/her to be the right path. To many, the first consideration is 'how much can I earn doing this?' and in many cases, it doesn't look promising that which your heart tells you to do. It is a wrong philosophy. It pays more,not necessarily in monetary terms, when you "follow your bliss" as Buddha said.

> *The cost of not following your heart is spending the rest of your life wishing you did.*
>
> *---Unknown---*

So here is the other truth you may want to know; if you do what you love to do, money will find you anyway. When you are in a field that you were meant to be, you will be having an unmatched passion that begets creativity and tenacity; both of which are very essential ingredients in your path to the TOP! Also it is important to know that you may have all the money without satisfaction, no happiness, no feeling of fulfillment. Following your passion will make you feel, look and live much better, happier and healthier.

The other approach is, starting where you are, could you possibly see how much value you are adding to the society and set something bigger for your legacy? That is, suppose, for example, you are an accountant in a supermarket. Are you able to figure out how much contribution you are doing to the society and even see the bigger picture and some contribution you could possibly make in that industry? Perhaps even writing a book about your subject to share your experience with others, making an impeccable career and even teaching people this accounting or even contributing to a curriculum? And what if you are a driver? Could you work on yourself to be the best driver that ever existed and even set up a school to help others learn how to drive skilfully and ethically? How about becoming the best driver who ever lived! Also, in politics, could you be a politician who contributed the most to positive changes and made the world a better place to live in and thus your spirit remains immortal in the hearts of your people? All these take courage and conviction over and above passion

> *Follow your heart and intuition. They somehow already know what you truly want to become. Everything else is secondary.*
>
> *---Steve Jobs---*

and purpose. You can do it!

Now, that could be another way to pick your life purpose, if, and only if, you are able to derive considerable passion doing that which you currently do. Else, go the other way; identifying your true purpose and going for it.

Obtaining Fulfillment

Kindly allow me to ask you a very personal question. A question that sounds trivial and easy but still seems not to have an obvious answer. Here we go; what does success really mean to you? Just take a couple of minutes to ponder over this because failure to get a good meaning that makes sense to you means you probably will not come across success and thus will not be happy either. Another related question is, do you really feel you are living or you are just passing time on earth awaiting the next world (if it exists)? There is a phrase I heard often, back in the village, and, to an extent, must have affected me. Remember it is true that your background has some bearing also, at least to a certain degree, to your level of success. Many people used to just exist; saying all the times, "*we're just getting by, a day at a time as long as we can get something for the stomach*." People simply trying to get by the day and call it a day; just trying to pass the day, get some food in the stomach and reach the night, "*escort with sleep*" so the following day can come and the routine goes on. It is pathetic! With such an attitude, miracles do not happen.

Having read this book up to this page, you sure cannot be in that category. You are doing something great; working towards making your life better. For this, I congratulate you. But have you understood, now, what success means to you? Have you, now, appreciated life and feel like you are living rather than surviving? Someone once said, "if you do not know what you can do with your limited life here on earth, how would you expect to be given an unlimited one in the hereafter!"

> *Success is the progressive realization of a predetermined worthy ideal.*
>
> *---Earl Nightingale---*

We have talked at length about life's purpose in the previous sections. It is necessary that we define success and successful living, at least from a perspective that can be helpful to you and me. That is the reason we now speak of *fulfillment*. My meaning of success can be different from yours and that is fine! We are different and think differently! Your dream is not mine and may not be the dream of your neighbor. What makes sense to you may not make sense to someone else. And part of the big problem in our society is that we have let other people define success for us and classify ourselves as, perhaps, failures without realizing that someone else's standard or definition does not have to become ours.

We must each learn to give our own definition of success

and what it will mean for us to be successful; Living Our Dreams! Good! Our Dreams and not someone else's. Your own dreams. That means, we must also be tolerant enough not to judge others according to our own standards. Part of the reason I could not hold any grudge with my dad for not paying my school fees and not showing much concern for many things that society considered important, was my ability to realize that we could be judging success on different scales. His idea of success, that kept amusing me, could be to 'live full today, make merry and have little concern for tomorrow'. I figured out that he probably was living according to the biblical book of Ecclesiastes 1:2; “vanity of vanities, everything is vanity”, while my view was proper education and financial security for the family and being helpful to the society in matters of education, economic empowerment and spirituality. So what could it mean to you? There is no right or wrong answer! All are dependent on your heart and calling.

If we were in a football match, success would simply mean scoring goals more than the opponent within the stipulated time period. This is true for most games. Apparently, it is not very far from life itself. We must have goals we want to achieve with our lives before we finish our earthly pilgrimage. And this is what gives life its meaning. It is what brings in fulfillment. Just like a footballer who has scored a goal feels greatly fulfilled. A good question to ask ourselves is, what is it that we would like to be remembered for! Or what would we want to achieve with our lives? How do we want to contribute to humanity? As Robin Sharma puts it in his book, *The Monk Who Sold His Ferrari*, "..at the deathbed, the last thing that people would ever wish is that they spent a little more time at workplace." What contribution would you want to make? What is important for you in this life?

CAUTION! Do not read this book just to finish. You will not get the rewards it is intended to give you. Do not just pass these questions as if you are reading a newspaper or racing to be paid for completing the book. That is one reason many people read books and stay the same. It would be better for you to even just take a paragraph and ponder over it enough in order to soak every nugget of wisdom therein. So, I suggest, understand the questions put to you in the preceding paragraphs and answer them. Answer them to yourself. Put them in your notebook and keep pondering over them. It is going to be a great key to your breakthrough. You may choose to share them with your spouse or a faithful confidante, like a mentor. Your life is going to change in a massive way. Trust me!

Listen to your heart,
it harbors sacred things.
Give from your heart;
Abundance it brings.
Pray through your heart;
guidance in need.
Follow your heart,
It knows how to lead.

---Paul Mark Sutherland---

I remember when I first attended a major team building retreat over a decade ago. During one night as we were crowded around the bonfire, eagerly and thoughtfully responding to thought-provoking questions from our brilliant instructors, I got lucky to arrive at a mega moment of truth! Here is one of the most intriguing questions that was being asked to every participant. This question has contributed greatly in changing/shaping my life to what it is today. It went something like this;

"Imagine that you died 10 years ago, having lived up to age 80. Imagine people have come to your 10th anniversary. You are listening to them, from wherever you are, talking about you and your life. Each one of them seem to be in agreement about some of the truths on how you affected their lives and your contributions in the society at large. What is it that you can hear them say about you?"

Take a moment to read the question through again, digest

and understand it. Then make it a question to yourself. Personalize it and try your best to give it an answer. An answer that comes from within you. Not from your mind, but from your heart. Ensure you are in total agreement with the answer you are giving; that it resonates well with your spirit. See yourself in the very act of doing what you are suggesting in your answer. After all this, look at yourself; your thoughts and activities, and find out if you are on the right track to achieving that particular goal. Note that this particular answer could be a hint into what your life purpose could be; the reason you were created. The reason you were born. And, perhaps, what success should mean to you.

Perhaps you may not like to hear people to talk much about the size of your house, nature of your home, or any material thing about you, but rather something more meaningful to the society; a general contribution to mankind that made life better. Perhaps Bill Gates will want to hear people talk about how he managed to make computers available to ordinary people and revolutionized the lifestyle, not much about how much money he made. And, if you ask me, it is that path of finding meaning and fulfillment that causes him, I mean Bill Gates, to now get involved in more charity issues than ever. Warren Buffet likewise; doing more good for many people with his monetary power.

If you get something that you want to be remembered for, that, my friend, forms your bigger goal in life; your legacy. It is the destination you want to aspire for, and the life you want to create for yourself. Ensure it is crystal clear in your mind and start writing your story. Every day, you have to move cinch by cinch towards that particular goal. Because every day forms part of your story. And no one knows how much time is left for them to accomplish the task at hand. That implies that if you have not started, you are late! Better start today. Start now, where you are and with what you have. Believe me, you can still do it! Live Your Dream!

In my own understanding, I concur with Earl Nightingale, John C Maxwell plus a few other philosophers that, success is the ***progressive*** realization of a ***predetermined*** worthy ideal. This predetermined worthy ideal has a lot to do with your life's purpose. You must be on the way towards realizing it, bit by bit, and thus building your legacy upon it. In the words of John C. Maxwell, success is:

1. Identifying your purpose in life
2. Progressively growing yourself and realizing that purpose to the max and
3. Sowing seeds that benefit others.

That legacy part is very central to your living. This is the sowing of seeds for others to reap. It is the planting of trees under whose shades you will not sit, the building of bridges you will never cross. Every single day you are at work, carrying out activities in your life, you will be realizing that you are, in a way, little by little, contributing towards your legacy, whether negatively or positively. Every day is a chapter in the book of your life; an episode in your movie where you're the star. Unless you are doing something really odd, this realization will make you to be very happy doing your work. It therefore makes you feel happy and satisfied. It has not much relationship with how much money you have in your bank account, but much to do with how much joy is in your heart. It makes you feel and believe that you are now starting to Live Your Dream!

> *He who has a why to live for can bear almost any how*
>
> *---Friedrich Nietzsche---*

Therefore, for anyone who wants to live a highly fulfilled life, who wants to be always happy and excited to wake up and go to work, to live a highly rewarding life both materially and emotionally, one must have a life purpose and work at it; realizing it bit by bit and moving slowly but surely towards the legacy he/she wants to leave. And if you ask me, that is one major reason some people seem to be doing better; healthier, happier and looking younger.

Personally, I consider my goal in life to be that of teaching people how to Live their Dreams. How to achieve greatness. To uplift people emotionally and to share with them, who are less informed, who think that achievement or happier living is a matter of good fortune or a reserve for particular people, that they may realize that they too have a chance. My dream has been to empower and equip over one million people with ideas and skills that enable them to realize their true worth, their dreams and thus assisting many more. In writing this book which is now in your hands, in part, I am Living my Dream! It is natural for me to educate people, to share the knowledge I have acquired through observation and analysis over the years; from my personal life and those of others. GOD naturally endowed me with the gifts and abilities towards this mission by providing me the natural curiosity into understanding, contemplative and discernment abilities, a scientific mind, academic prowess, ability for public speaking and all necessary tools to accomplish this mission; even guiding my path towards what to study in college, jobs to take and putting such desires in my heart. I am alive when I am sharing knowledge and motivating people. And I am very grateful for the time you are spending with me here, being part of this noble mission. You too have a mission and you are well equipped for it!

> *Your purpose in life is to find your purpose and to give your whole heart and soul to it.*
>
> *---Gautama Buddha---*

Chapter 2

DETERMINATION

Backed By Burning Desire

Whatever it takes

Are you really serious you want to Live Your Dream? Then failure must never overtake you! James Allen, in his book, As a Man Thinketh, said,

"The human Will, that force unseen,
The offspring of a deathless Soul,
Can hew a way to any goal,
Though walls of granite intervene.
That's the attitude; Whatever it takes!"

Here is a story you are probably familiar with, perhaps into greater details than me. I got this format recently in on social media and found it exciting. Here it goes:

- At age 5 his Father died.
- At age 16 he quit school.

- At age 17 he had already lost four jobs.
- At age 18 he got married.
- Between ages 18 and 22, he was a railroad conductor and failed.
- He joined the army and washed out there.
- He applied to join law school was rejected.
- He became an insurance sales man and failed again.
- At age 19 he became a father.
- At age 20 his wife left him and took their baby daughter.
- He became a cook and dishwasher in a small café.
- He failed in an attempt to kidnap his own daughter, and eventually he convinced his wife to return home.
- At age 65 he retired.
- On the 1st day of retirement he received a cheque from the Government for $105.
- He felt that the Government was saying that he couldn't provide for himself.

- He decided to commit suicide, it wasn't worth living anymore; he had failed so much.
- He sat under a tree writing his will, but instead, he wrote what he would have accomplished with his life. He realized there was much more that he hadn't done. There was one thing he could do better than anyone he knew. And that was how to cook.
- So he borrowed $87 against his cheque and bought and fried up some chicken using his recipe, and went door to door to sell them to his neighbors in Kentucky.
- He met with 1,009 Nos before finally landing to a YES! for his chicken recipe!

Remember at age 65 he was ready to commit suicide. But at age 88 Colonel Sanders, founder of Kentucky Fried Chicken (KFC) Empire was a billionaire and till now his business is still expanding like never before around the globe!

What's your excuse?

Research shows that one of the greatest causes of failure is the tendency to 'quit when the going gets tough'. One who is willing to succeed in a given venture must wear this particular attitude; 'whatever it takes!' No kidding! Somehow nature, in her immense wisdom, tends to hide from us all the possible problems and difficulties we are going to meet on the way. Before we start, it only tells us much of the great rewards that we are bound to achieve; painting rosy pictures of what is possible for us. This is a good 'trick', if I may call it, because without it, no one would really get started. The few who normally take this road would be scared to death if only they had a glimpse of the reality that awaits. Many people who have succeeded, succeeded not only because they had the courage to get started, but also because they had the staying power, the '*whatever it takes*' attitude, and thus persisted to the finish line. We know from testimonies, as many successful people confess, that had they known what they would have to go through, perhaps they would not have started at all. It is that scary! You therefore must have a tough mental attitude; something I call 'mental toughness' and a certain level of determination that knows not the meaning of giving up. Somehow, nature has a way to (even) 'bend rules' and obey him who has refused to let go. That is the way it is!

Thinking about this particular attitude, one of the best examples ever known to mankind is Thomas Edison. When he was looking for a solution to electrical lighting, he demonstrated that the only way to fail is to quit! You probably know this story well enough too. He was able to withstand just over 10,000 points of failure. That is 10,000 opportunities to quit, but he did not allow himself to quit! When asked at the end how possible it is that a man would go through such staggering number of failures and still disappoint failure by 'failing to quit', what did he say?

"I did not fail! I simply discovered over ten thousand ways of how NOT to make a bulb" was his response! What an amazing attitude! Reminds me of the statement of apostle Paul in his 2nd letter to the Corinthians (in the scriptures) where he says, "it is when I'm weak that I'm strong." Look at the paradox in that statement.

> *I have missed more than 9000 shots in my career. I have lost almost 300 games. On 26 occasions, I have been entrusted to take the game-winning shot and missed I have failed over and over and over again in my life. And that's why I succeed .*
>
> *---Michael Jordan---*

When we used to hold monthly business meetings for our Network Marketing business, we would use projectors to run presentations. We would borrow a projector from the company. This particular projector would be so difficult at times that we would fail to use it literally for an entire session. But that would never happen easy. My upline director's upline would keep tweaking it and trying it for the whole session. I learnt a lot from this particular gentleman, who actually had been my friend from the time I joined college till this date. He is still one of my business mentors even as I write this material. He never gave up on anything!

No wonder he would succeed at anything he touched! Even the time we were in college, trying to connect the Public Address Systems, he would be at it and continue until it either works or the service ends; whichever would come first! That is what I call 'whatever it takes attitude'.

When we started doing our own trainings, learning and practicing Network Marketing on our own without our upline President Team Member, after falling out with him on the methodology of doing the business, we were determined to try all that would be possible until we would find success that we were looking for. Our team was mostly comprised of college graduates who were full of enthusiasm and could dare to research and succeed at anything! We were clear about what we were looking for. Having learnt that most people who had been in business in our region were always quitting at some point, we discovered there could be something wrong. During one of our trials and experiments with the system, this mentor of mine, Pascal, said to me; “now we are free. We shall keep tweaking it and tuning it just like a TV aerial when looking for signal until we find what works and how it works.” Those were the days of analogue broadcasting technology. That statement made a lot of sense to me. I still use it till now. No quitting! Just trying until we find what works. I later formed my own systems which, till now, serves me well; simple, duplicable and scalable! You must keep trying until you succeed! No letting go. I heard Les Brown saying that we must keep telling ourselves:

"No matter how hard it is or how hard it's gonna be, I'm going to make it!"

Pascal is a true demonstration of this attitude and has been my great teacher in this field! I thank GOD for him.

Determination always sees the way. It is always powered by possibilities and hope. Hope which "does not disappoint" according to the apostle Paul's epistle to the Romans 5:5. This is a way of thinking; a system of belief, a culture to acquire. It helps to know that one with such an attitude shall rejoice because success shall surely come to him/her at an acceptable time.

> *"..we even boast of our afflictions,*
> *knowing that affliction produces endurance*
> *and endurance, proven character*
> *and proven character, hope*
> *and hope does not disappoint.."*
>
> ----Romans 5:3-5----

The Role of Faith

Faith is worth almost everything! If you could put it on one side of a balancing scale and find something else on the other side to make it balance, perhaps you would realize that very few things can be compared to faith. And it begins with you! That is, faith in yourself! It is a very indispensable attribute in anyone who is matching to greatness. The first time I attended a presentation for a Network Marketing business, I heard that one of the qualifications for success in the business was Faith. Faith in self, faith in the business, faith in the products, *et cetera.* I had to believe in myself in order to make it in this business. It did not make sense for me then until I hit a snag. That's the time I went back to the requirements in order to evaluate myself and reflect on the lessons. It became crystal clear. I had not bought the concept. I had not really been sold into it and thus did not have ample faith, even 'as tiny as a mustered seed', to keep me growing. The truth dawned on me. No Faith, No Success!

Whatever you think you are, you really are (or at least you are becoming). Therefore, W. Clement Stone stipulated: whether you think you can or you can't, either way you are right! This means that people who win are people who believe in themselves and thus they expect to win. The converse is normally true. You must see yourself winning in order to win. You must have seen yourself a loser in order to lose. No in between. No chance!

The question about believing in yourself, now that you could be thinking about it, could be, "what if I believe I cannot? Would it be possible to believe otherwise?" And that is what I am here to tell you that you can actually change your belief. It is possible to influence your mind, logically and methodically, to believe what you want it to believe. If it were not possible, there, naturally, would not have been a reason for this book; let alone those many others in the streets. How do you do it?

> *You can't sell what you can't buy. You must first be sold into your product and believe in it before you can sell it.*
>
> *---Otieno Paul-Peter---*

Looking for solutions to unlock my business, I kept reading books and pondering. Then one evening a business leader came from a neighboring country, Uganda. He was doing great and so I honestly respected him. I heard he was going to have a talk one evening and so it was only prudent that I should attend. He, started by saying.. "if your business is not growing, stop and ask yourself whether you really believe in your business. Do you really believe that you are in the right business? Do you believe in yourself?..." That's the point I remembered the issue of qualifications I was given earlier. I realized that my level of faith was not impressive. I had to do something and do it fast! I had to influence myself to the new beliefs. My business was a total reflection of me. If I had no faith in what I was doing, in my business, in my products, in my economy, I had no chance! So I went out to look for how to get this faith, more so being a scientifically inclined person who did not imagine success could have a faith angle, and discovered how it works.

My formula, therefore, of doing this normally entails some form of reasoning. It's fairly simple! First, let us start with the question:- is what you want to do doable? Most of the times you will find the answer to be an absolute YES. Let me give you a story.

When I joined the university, my first few months were not exciting at all! The physics units were extremely tough. Most of those units assumed the mathematics units which we were supposed to have done in order to make them bearable. Some of the mathematics units that were even supposed to be done in second semester were already being applied here. Many of my classmates were depressed! People would run to the library very early in the morning to read and research. This would continue, literally, the whole day unless there was a lecture. The practicals were equally not encouraging at all. Some people gave up and transferred to other courses. In fact, most of us would go to class to sign the attendance list and take notes if possible; not to understand. One of our lecturers, being frank with us, advised that we have to choose between either taking notes or trying to understand. But because it would not be possible to understand at that time within the class period, he advised that taking notes and then trying to understand later would be ideal. It was during this 'trying times' that a relative called and asked how I was doing in college. I lamented in very many words how tough life was with academics. After patiently listening to all my groaning and testimony of torture, he simply asked, “are there other people who have done the exact same thing you are doing” and you can guess my answer! “So it is doable”, he said, "you can do it". I got the sense. I embraced that attitude of I can do it! I bought the first installment of faith in myself!

Therefore, one way to convince your mind is by asking, has it been done before? If it has been done, then it can be done and thus, you too can do it! Though this is not an absolute test, since at times you will have to do what hasn't been done before, but it is a starting point and would increase your level of confidence. And if someone else can do it, why not you! You too can do it, and, perhaps, much better! Have faith in yourself.

> *Believe in yourself! Have faith in your abilities. Without a humble but reasonable confidence in your own powers, you cannot be successful or happy.*
>
> *---Dr. Norman Vincent Peale---*

Now, sometimes you have no evidence that it can be done because no one ever did it. Here, all you need to do is to consult your heart. It will hardly disappoint you. If deep in your heart you realize the urge to go ahead and do something, it means you can do it. Do not listen to your mind or your logics. Just your heart. Do not listen to what others say or how others judge you. They are never accurate at all. Besides, some of the statements they would use to describe you are driven by envy and selfishness. For my case, convincing myself that I could go to the university took the second option. I had not seen anyone go from our village, more so one whom I could identify with. It was a matter of listening to my heart. It is very important at this point that you do not allow your mind to rest or focus on those negative thoughts that discourage you from taking action.

I was so convinced and determined that I told myself I would do whatever it takes! According to me, it would take even 10 years; it would take me going to look for something to do to generate income that would be sufficient to pay my school fees and finally after passing exams to look for money for the college fees. That is the university. My little knowledge, then, was that if it is difficult getting fees for secondary education, it would be many times more difficult to pay university fee. But that would not stop me anyway. I had the determination with me and I was unstoppable!

I set out to go fishing in order to gather some little money. Fishing had been a lucrative business in our region and the sole source of livelihood for many people. So for the first time I set out with some friends to the other side of the lake, a place called *Seme*, to fish and earn some money. After staying there for about three weeks, no results were forthcoming. Nothing to smile about! If you really want to know what apostle Peter and his companions went through when they were found by Jesus of Nazareth, having tried the whole night to catch fish in vain, you can ask me! In the words of Donald Trump, the 45th president of the United States, “it was not exactly fun.” For some reason all the fish agreed, somehow, to (perhaps) attend some retreat at an unknown location and our efforts were fruitless. It is one of the hardest experiences you can go through. I figured out that besides being far from home, risking my life in the task of fishing, nothing much was going to come out of it, at least that soon. You may want to call this 'quitting'. But that's not true! My mission was looking for fees and going back to school, not fishing. So, against the wish and advice of my comrades, I chose to go back home. Some of them jeered and even confessed that no one ever went there to do the fishing and returned to school. I did not listen.

Having returned home, I engaged in a few other types of fishing, my known trade, with some other friend, and the story was not any different, only riskier health-wise; walking in very cold waters early in the morning, moving in water-weeds that scratch the body and most of the times when the sun comes up you feel really terrible and long to stay in the water instead. My body was cracked and close to that of a lizard, my legs and nails were colored. Something told me that if I continued like this, I would even get some of the ailments associated with water and that would be difficult bearing in mind that I was not earning money that would take care of my hospital bills. No one would take that responsibility either. At least as far as my experience could tell. I, therefore, left to go start a hawking business in town. It was safer and a little simpler. It entailed going round with sweets and chewing gum which I later dropped and started selling boiled eggs. By the way, I was the first person to peddle boiled eggs in my hometown, Kendu Bay. Even today whenever I go back home, I see someone who started in my days still doing it! Isn't that amazing? Decades later, the guy is still on the same trade doing the same things the same way! Perhaps it is his call. Call it faith in his product?

> *Faith is taking the first step even when you don't see the whole staircase.*
>
> *---Martin Luther King, Jnr.---*

I would love to tell you that I finally earned enough money to pay my school fees. But I would be lying. The money I was earning was as little as chicken milk. It could not do more than putting food in my stomach. But, yes, I must admit that one of the greatest skills that I lacked in my life and thus contributed massively in retarding my success is *Personal Finance Management.* I was good at making money but not very good at managing it. You cannot be successful without this skill! I'll talk about this later. I did not give up my dream, I did not listen to people who would discourage me. Some relatives, because I seemed to be suffering, advised that I should go to my maternal uncle's place and live with them. In my view, that was not a very good advice. It would not help me to be in school. Besides, I had learnt from experience that if anything good had to happen to me, it is up to me to take the full responsibility and make it happen; not to entrust someone else with it. Thank GOD this revelation came to me earlier. It has helped me a great deal. If you still want to expect your help to come from others, I pity you. It will do you a lot good to start taking responsibility.

With all these meanders in my journey to pursuing education, I never let go. I was determined. I had faith in myself. Faith from the bottom of my heart, not from others. No matter what you are pursuing, this is my advise, you may keep changing the course but do not change the goal or vision. You will win if you don't quit! Whatever it takes, believe in yourself!

Your Heart, Your Guide

> *The more you trust your intuition, the more empowered you become, the stronger you become, the happier you become.*
>
> *---Gisele Bundchen---*

Over the years, I have drawn a few very important conclusions. To me, they form the very fundamentals of successful living. One of them is this; trust what your heart tells you. Your heart, in most important decisions, is superior to your mind. Your heart can listen to things beyond your ear, see things beyond your eyes, feel things beyond your senses. Here is my other perspective; three things will hardly disappoint you; your heart, your conscience and, your intuition. The only problem is that I do not know if the three things are, in truth, one and the same thing. But I suspect they are very distinct. As you empower them, they respond more and more accurately and much faster. You empower them by use.

Now, the foregoing statement must not be taken blindly. In order to make it clearer and do it justice, let me mention the following: at the moments when you really need counsel, logic is good, but full of discouragements. People can advise you, but not so reliably, more so when it comes to following your dream. You are going to understand it better as we continue with examples and real life stories. For now, just remember, trust your instincts, your heart, your conscience. Use them more and more and you will become much better, over time, at using them more accurately.

The law of Use and Disuse is very important for your success. It states that **whatever you don't use, you lose**. To the best of my knowledge, it is one of those immutable laws of nature. If you do not use your mind, you will lose it! If you do not use your hand, you will equally lose it. It is true for everything. Just look around and notice that even if you do not put your car, house or whatever it may be, to use, you are more likely to lose it. It is that simple. It applies to everyone and everything equally. So by using your senses, you empower them, they respond better and faster because that is the way they grow. Therefore, learn how to employ your heart, intuition and conscience. Put them into use constantly and you will be amazed at the positive results.

Trust the trio and follow them. Little success comes otherwise.

Noticed in the story of KFC above that colonel Sanders finally decided to do what he loved doing most, cooking chicken, and therein the billions he was looking for throughout his life popped up? True success and fulfillment follows passion, and that comes when we use less of logic and more of instinct! It was, surely, not the most logical thing for Col.Sanders to do; spending his little retirement fortune in trying to look for gold in the kitchen at a ripe old age. But something inside him told him to do it despite the odds, and he did it!

The other thing to note is that he was able to withstand 1,009 rejections! What a staggering number, you may think! How did he do it? It is because he did what he loved. When you follow your passion, failure is more bearable, creativity sets in and the attitude of determination is quite practical.

How to Solve Problems

Even in following your passion, it is still possible to die trying without ever achieving the significant success you are dreaming about. You will be better off because you, at least, tried and failed. You will also be much happier and fulfilled. It is better to try and fail than to fail to try. Failing to try is a more serious failure! And when you get started, when you give it a shot, you give it your heart and put your all in it. But what else could hinder your success despite your enthusiasm and determination? There could be a very thin line between determination and insanity. More so if you consider the popular phrase, insanity is doing the same thing, the same way over and over again and expecting a different result. So what next?

> *Education is the most powerful weapon which you can use to change the world.*
>
> *---Nelson Mandela---*

It is my belief that ignorance is the greatest liability of mankind. As has often been said, 'people perish due to lack of knowledge'. How true! Almost every pain that man goes through can be avoided with proper knowledge, or, at least, can be overcome with relative ease if only we chose to learn. But guess what? Not many people like seeking knowledge. On the contrary, very few people have the desire to learn. Let alone to read. This is a big tragedy and shall always be one of the greatest stumbling blocks. I congratulate you for your effort. By reading these lines, you are proving to be among the few who read. You are on your way to the TOP!

Your future is, first and foremost, determined by what you know! Your philosophy! If you have little knowledge, or should I say little information, your future can only be bleak at best. You must study. Self study. Today, getting information does not take a genius. All it requires is willingness to obtain it. Your knowledge is very important in forming your belief system, that ends up in your subconscious, to drive you to the future that you hold in your mind. Working on your knowledge-base is a fundamental thing. When you stop reading, you stop growing. Reading could be your best weapon in your quest to realize the greatness that is within you.

Quoting from a renown speaker, Les Brown, "Life is a fight for territory. The moment you stop fighting for what you want, whatever you do not want automatically takes over." If you are going to be in a position to Live Your Dream, you will have to choose to be a perpetual learner. Having an attitude of a learner is a great attribute for successful people. You can't know it all! It is actually when you think you have known it all that you need to learn even the more. In the school of success, there is no graduation. Knowledge is necessary in order to solve problems. Here are my suggested steps in problem solving; a strategy I often present to different audiences. They are in form of questions to self:

a:What really is the problem?

At this point, one should try to be clear about what the problem really is. Let us take for example you are in the business of selling sweets and you do not sell as much as you want or as much as you should. Take time to ask yourself what the problem really is. Is it your knowledge of the product, market, or could it be timing? What could it be? Notice that this starts by accepting that there is a problem.

That you really do have a problem. Not blaming someone else for it. Denial does not help. One must come to terms with the truth and accept, if it exists, that there is a problem; big or small. And so after acknowledging that, you try to figure out what it could be. You try to establish the root-cause.

When I first ventured into direct selling, I had no real background in the field, having come from a school of science and landing into an ICT industry as a technical support person, it was really hard for me. I had done hawking 10 years before, but that was a different terrain. No structure at all, no need for prospecting. Just exposing the products and displaying them. But this was a different ball-game. I noticed that nothing much was happening in my business. I was literally stuck! No progress. I could not achieve my monthly targets as required by the company and that meant no earnings.

For quite awhile I got into a state which I later called 'Limbo'. This is a state, I have come to learn, almost every business person reaches; more so in Network Marketing. It is a time you lose enthusiasm, doubts creep in and you ask yourself critical questions. It is the time when the honeymoon is over and reality sets in. The cozy picture you initially had in your mind disappears and you wonder whether you really made the right decision getting started anyway. It is at this stage when you start hearing the sounds of the people who warned you and logic sets in. All of a sudden you stop listening to your heart and start rationalizing things. It is a sorry state and many people quit at this point or look for alternative ventures and lose focus.

Unfortunately this stage may come more than a few times in your journey and you may actually, without looking for solution, fail to have the appropriate muscles to pull through. Stuck in the mud, I tell you. I was there and have been there a few more times. This is the reason I often say, one always starts or joins a venture at least twice. The first time, you join with your heart. The second and other times, you will have to join with all your mind as well. Just like a marriage relationship. Indeed, it is a marriage relationship. You get to marry your work or get married to your work, or business if you prefer.

> *If I had 60 minutes to solve a problem, I would spend 55 minutes defining it and 5 minutes to solve it.*
>
> *---Albert Einstein---*

It was at this point that I stopped and asked myself; "what could be the problem?" I got into a blame game and blamed most things around, at least in my mind; "I think the products are too expensive.., may be it is the economy.., may be it's the time I am lacking..".., etc. In the long run, after being true to myself, after looking around and seeing other people in the same company, using the same plan, same products, same price-list, same training, same location, same government ... and yet doing a thousand times better, then I noted the problem was neither the industry, nor the company, the products, the government… It was me! The problem was within me. In other words, I was the problem. It did not require me to use any complex analytical equations to figure out or to prove this fact. As Muslim brothers like to put it, 'say what is truth even if it is bitter.' Well, that was the bitter truth. I'm glad I accepted it.

> *Running away from a problem does not solve a problem.*
>
> *---Otieno Paul-Peter---*

Sometimes you will not clearly see the problem. You may have certain limitations. But once you have accepted there must be a problem, you may want to share with someone else; a mentor, a coach, a more experienced person in the field, to help you identify what the problem could be. It is still fine.

b:What can I do?

Once you have identified where the problem is, perhaps it is somewhere else and not you, though in many cases it could be you, it is now time to ask yourself what you, as an individual, can do about your situation. Remember, the buck always stops with you. If you do not take action, possibly no one else will. Even if you sought the counsel of a mentor, nothing much happens if you do not act on it. Many people, unfortunately, usually ask what other people ought to do.

They want and expect someone else to do something about the prevailing problem. That is where blames are born. That is the time someone thinks; may be my uncle should pump in some more money here, perhaps the government should scrap these regulations or taxes, may be my partners are not doing enough, if only this weather could be hotter for longer,...the list is endless. They resent and get into the wrong mode of blame game. Like I did. Blaming everyone and everything else but me. This is the worst thing you can do for yourself! Never allow yourself to get to the level of complaining and blaming others. If you do, you are trading your dream. You will learn more about this as you continue to read.

The moment you have identified the problem or problems and accepted responsibility, find what you can do about it and do it quickly. Get on because you do not have all the time. And one of the few things you can do in solving problems follows in the question below.

c:What Can I Read?

Finding answers to life or business problems is not a straight forward affair. It takes the same old effort and determination. But as long as you truly have a BURNING DESIRE to Live Your Dream, it is very doable and the journey very exciting. You become, to an extent, a researcher. You will have to read somethings on your own and figure out the solutions. You must accept that some problems can be fairly unique in your situation, and thus the bit for figuring out from the clues you may get from the books.

At times, solution will come as a flush of insight as long as you keep pondering over the problem and concentrating your mind on the exact outcome you expect. Even the most difficult problems are solved in this manner. Persistent and consistent reading and thinking. That is what others call mediating on the problem. Solution can come even in your sleep or during a church service or anywhere. It will just strike you. But you must put in effort, at least mentally, to realize this. People like John D. Rockefeller and Henry Ford used this method to solve their complex business problems. This method is still effective today.

In my case, it was my inability to sell which was hindering my progress and stealing my dream. I could hardly sell a product. Money only comes when we sell, remember, no matter the trade you are involved in. And a business without money, is like a human being without blood. It has no life! So after noticing that I was the problem, and knowing exactly that in order to live my dream of Financial Freedom I had to learn and master how to sell, I knew exactly what to do; learn how to sell, **whatever it takes!**

Armed with determination that knows no quitting, with a consuming desire to achieve my goals and dreams, I immediately immersed myself into reading and studying and practicing. That was my dawn into the self help industry. I read quite a good number of books, listened to different speakers and trainers in the field and practiced as much as I could. Do not get me wrong, I still keep studying and learning. As I already mentioned, in the school of success, we do not graduate. And besides, I had declared myself a student of life for life; always studying and learning the ways of life; ways that produce success. I have a great passion for learning and sharing knowledge. That is how I became a trainer, a business coach teaching business skills, and a public speaker; studying, practicing and seeing what works and what does not work, and why.

> *Seeing much, suffering much and studying much are the three pillars of learning.*
>
> *---Benjamin Disraeli---*

I became very good at selling and this immediately started showing in my business. My products started moving and up to now I have not had any difficulties achieving my monthly targets and shall probably never. I love selling so much that I have since taught many people how to sell and compiled manuals on the same. The same principles I did learn, employed and still use, I have passed on to many people in the business world. Today I can afford to say, 'I Love Selling'. That was unimaginable then. It has become one of my pet subjects. Besides solving sales problem, I had to ensure I keep the customers I acquired. From practice, analysis and some sort of iteration, plus studies, I have kept my customer-bases very solid. That was the beginning of my interest in training business. Every time I see a business having issues, I know there is a problem with some of those essential skills. It reached a point that whenever I even went to a restaurant, a shop or a stall, it was easy for me to figure out whether the business was likely to collapse in a few months or prosper eventually.

Dear reader, you too, can solve any problem by reading about it and listening to people who are doing it, who have done it and succeeded. You just need to make a decision on how to keep your learning curve positive. Keeping the attitude of learning and seeking solutions. Have fun doing it. “All skills are learnable”, said Brian Tracy, “..and success leaves tracks”. So if you know what you really want, you can always maneuver your way and find the right solutions for your problem without listening to rumors or surrendering. It is possible!

d:Whom Can I Ask?

This is the final stage, according to me. Asking. At this time, you already know exactly what your problem is and the type of solution you are looking for. It is important to know that even when you are reading, it is like asking because someone wrote that book. Even by searching on the Internet, you are still asking. But strictly speaking, here I actually mean going to some real person and asking questions. Again it is important to know the right person to ask. This solution is number one strategy to a great majority; they simply do not want to research. They hate reading and studying. They want quick fixes! If you hurriedly ask, more so wrong people, you will most likely end up with wrong answers.

> *We cannot solve our problems with the same level of thinking that created them.*
>
> *---Albert Einstein---*

Notice that advice is the cheapest commodity trading around. Everyone gives advice; including failures and fools. Well, it is not that failures should not give advice. They should. Perhaps they will assist you in avoiding a pitfall. You only need to know their honesty. They should teach you what can make you fail rather than what can make you succeed. More so if they are really analytical. But it is important to know the type of failure we are talking about. A failure, in this context, is someone who either failed to start or failed to finish. He or she could also be someone who is getting the results you don't want to get, or who is not happy with his/her life.

Ensure the person you are asking is the right person to ask. Many people ask the people they know. The people they trust or love. Trust is not the only qualification here; knowledge is! If it is a medical problem, ask a medical practitioner, whether a friend, relative or whoever, it does not matter. Just ask. If it is a building problem, you could ask a builder, an architect or a civil engineer. That is, someone who is experienced in that field. If it is a business problem, you may not want to necessarily ask an MBA lecturer in a university. Ask a business person. Real life problems are solved by real life solutions. Not theories. And real life solutions come from experience. That is why when you are looking for a surgeon you do not want an intern to operate on you. Attend lectures, seminars, talks and workshops on the same. If it is selling, ask real sellers with experience; more so those with the results you would like to have. Your mother may not be the best person to ask unless she is doing exactly what you want to do. But guess whom we mostly run to for advice. Parents, religious leaders, teachers,...relatives among others. No wonder we hardly get solutions to our real-life problems. Sometimes it is because we want it free. We do not want to pay anything. So we often get advice at no pay which is worth no pay; not unless you're really lucky. You could be lucky to have mentors in the field to give it for free, though in many instances you may need to book for that meeting and spend some time with them, perhaps buying them lunch or coffee. So you pay in time or otherwise. Bottom-line, before you ask, know whom you are asking.

In short, identify the problem, get the root-cause, see what you can do about it, find something you can read, get someone you can ask. Almost all problems shall be solvable in this manner with a positive mindset.

Activity

All that you have learnt must now be put to practice. There is only one way to produce results using the knowledge you have acquired; activity! You must work! Knowledge is necessary. It is your game changer. It forms your philosophy. It determines how fast and how much you can succeed. It determines your attitudes too. But all that is useless without activities and that means your knowledge is a waste without activity. There is no difference between you and a book. Even a book knows the things you want to know. But a book really has no dreams while you do! So you must work yourself to your dream. Or is there a difference between one who reads and does not practice and one who does not read?

I have a formula that goes like this: R=T+A. I like talking about it because I am yet to find anything truer! 'R' stands for 'Results', 'T' stands for 'Thoughts' and 'A' stands for 'Activities'. Therefore Results equal Thoughts plus Activities! That is to say, what you get is determined by what you Think added to what you Do. If you only remember this, you will still be good to go and shall have a fair chance for success in your life. The formula summarizes all personal development. It is leadership. It is responsibility. Notice I

> *Your **R**esults are a function of your **T**houghts and your **A**ctivities. i.e. **R=T+A**.*
>
> *---Otieno Paul-Peter---*

start with Results? Yes! It is deliberate. It will help if you start with the end in mind; starting by knowing clearly what you want. That is the dream or goal, not withstanding what results mean to you.

If you look at the formula again, you realize that it does not talk about someone else, but you. It means that whenever you are getting the results that are not of your liking, whom do you blame? You are right. You! No one else! You must know that you are the source of all your results; from your thoughts and your activities. How the hell is that, you may ask? I shall explain it simply.

A student thinks for herself, 'I really must pass these exams. I have no choice.' Then she goes out and does whatever it takes; reading, revising, discussions, asking, praying and all that is necessary to do with. Finally, she expects to pass because she has done what she thinks is right and is pleased with herself. What happens when results are out? She has definitely passed the exams. The converse is equally true!

Whenever you want to change your results, ask yourself if there is anything you do not know or something you are not doing right and then comb it out. Do not blame anyone else. Perhaps I need to say, also, that your 'Thoughts' are determined by your level of knowledge and feelings. Your knowledge level is a subject of what you read, what you watch, whom you associate with and your attitude about learning. You have a choice, at any particular point in your life, to increase your knowledge and know more or know less.

Sometime back when the Government of Kenya decided to evict people from the forest reserves in order to conserve the natural forests which were being encroached and thus adversely affecting the climate, it was common knowledge that tree cutting was not good for the economy and society, but what did a politician looking for votes do, he went and told the forest dwellers that they must rise in arms and resist the eviction. That everyone knows that rains come from GOD and not from trees. You see? This type of thinking affected the locals and the effects are still evident. If you think rain simply comes from GOD, which it does, perhaps, and that forests have nothing to do with it (even as a precondition for GOD to give the rain), then what activities follow? Deforestation. Then? Adversity is the result. Your 'Thoughts', therefore, which is determined by your level of knowledge and your attitude of the mind, plus your 'Activities' shall bring your 'Results'. Even the results you have today can be traced to what you ever thought and what you did. It is because of this that Buddha said, "*thought in the mind hath made us. Whatever we think, we become.*"

If you want it, you can get it!

---Giants' Team Slogan---

By improving your knowledge level, you improve your thinking, you improve your problem solving ability, you improve your level of control of the process and thus results. You therefore have a better chance of Living Your Dream, and your determination ultimately pays dividends. This, therefore, is one of the points of determination. As you persist in following your passion and pursuing your dream, learning, practicing and evaluating your progress toward your predetermined *Worthy Ideal* form a big part of your activities.

It would be important to know that some of the activities will take place so naturally and effortlessly that you will hardly notice they were part of the process! They will be much more enjoyable than you think. That is possible only if you maintain a positive mindset. But remember, there is really nothing you cannot do! You can actually "do all things through Him who strengthens" you as the scripture says. That is to say, you really have whatever it takes to do what has to be done to obtain the results you want.

The Inner You, Role of Emotion

As I have said, part of what makes your thoughts is *what you know*. Your thoughts are composed of what you know and what you feel. We have talked about what you know, which is your philosophy; your level of knowledge. Let us touch a bit on this hot topic of FEELING. It could be one of the most important elements in unlocking your potential. I am about to invoke a law that will change your life completely, that is if you had not heard about it. If you will believe it, study it and start applying it. Lack of this knowledge is one of the greatest causes of the many predicaments that people meet in life. It is the cause for every success, every failure. It is the Master Key. It opens doors; whether to prosperity or to oblivion. This single key has put men and women in lofty places. It has sent people to 'hell'. It has caused people to marry the ones they love, it has broken families and built them too. It has brought money and opulence. Yes! It has brought poverty and misery as well.

If you use it well, it will help you. Like a double-edged sword, if you do not use it well, it will ruin you. You have actually been using it. Either in ignorance or with understanding. It is important to use it with proper understanding in order to make good use of it. Because you cannot, as you will see, avoid using it, it is constantly in operation and steering your life's destiny on a daily basis. Some call it luck; seeing one succeed, they attribute it all to luck. Others talk of fate; something unknown to us upon which we have no control. Well, perhaps it may be one or the other. At least in our minds and thoughts. But, is it really?

This mysterious attribute of mankind has been known for all ages, though it keeps being elusive and taking the form of a secret. It has been applied, knowingly or otherwise, but mostly knowingly, by the greatest of leaders, the greatest of sages, the greatest entrepreneurs. It has been woven in various forms of literature from of old. It is an absolute TRUTH of nature! An absolute LAW. A law of nature, again, very unbendable, perhaps, except, by GOD Himself.

You cannot halt it, you cannot run away from it, you cannot escape it, but you can cooperate with it. That cooperation, actually, is the only way to harness its powers to your advantage. But you can only cooperate with it positively when you have full knowledge on how it works and the full attributes of its nature. The very same knowledge, again, here reigns supreme. It is what you know.

> *There are no shortcuts to anywhere worth going.*
>
> *---Beverly Sills---*

Apparently, we have been talking about it throughout this book, without calling it by its real name. If you are keen enough, or if you are familiar with it, you already noticed it in the principles hitherto discussed. All great writings, in one way or the other allude to it; with or without full understanding.

If there is one single person who is in charge of your life, if there is one person who has the ability to direct your life to whichever direction, it is YOU! If you love your life as it is today, give yourself a pat on your back. You have been using the tool well. If you are not really happy with your life as it is today, you are on the right track. Feel happy because henceforth you are going to be aware of what is happening. Did I say it is easy? No! It is hard. Really hard! Perhaps the hardest labor you are going to engage in, more so at the start. But the whole life is hard and we do not expect anything good to be easy. As Margaret Ogolla once put it in her marvelous Novel, River and The Source, *"Nothing good comes easy. A good thing is worth every single struggle."* I take it that you have chosen to walk the narrow road to greatness and that is why you are reading this book. Here is the good news. You not only can do it, but you shall be able to do it and surely Live Your Dream! It is part of the reason for determination backed by burning desire.

Thoughts Become Things!

That is it! As you think, so you become! I would like you to take this statement very literally. That is because it is the TRUTH! Your THOUGHTS in your MIND have made you whom you are right now and the THOUGHTS you are thinking today are creating the future you are going to posses. This is a Law. It is one of the strangest laws that govern life. It is what has been referred to as The Strangest Secret, by Earl Nightingale, and it is not a secret anymore, though it keeps appearing as if it were! It has been called the Law of Attraction. Stated another way, *What You Think, You Become.*

Your success, therefore, must begin in your mind. Then it must descend to your heart. You must think success, in your heart, with your emotions, in order to become a success. We are calling it THINKING and FEELING.

FEELING part is the precondition. If you think, in your heart, you are going to succeed, you certainly will succeed. It is just a matter of time. If you can not see yourself succeeding, well, exactly what you see is what you are going to get. It is strange, but it is true! If you choose to doubt, it is going to help you doubt it because the principle still works; 'what you see (in your mind) and feel (in your heart) is what you get. What you think you become.'

It does not help to argue with the law. If you cannot comprehend it for now, just understand that it exists and it works. We shall have a few illustrations to make it simpler for you to understand and start using it consciously this very moment. Actually, as I have said, if you have been paying attention keenly from the time you started reading this book, absorbing the stories that have been related, then you should be able to notice this secret. It is this aspect of having it being mysteriously woven into the body of knowledge that makes it appear as if it is a secret and keeps it strange. For a start, just stay alert to the results you get in every situation and then dig back to your former feelings and see the relationship. You can do experiments on your own. Keep this in mind and try to see it in every story from now henceforth. Try it out in your day-to-day life. Make up something to help you experiment. Perhaps you start thinking of getting late for an appointment or closing a particular deal. See it in your mind and feel it. Imagine it has already happened and keep it in your mind as long as you can. The longer the better. Then forget about it and never think anything else to the contrary. Instead, keep busy with other things. You will be amazed!

The main tip here is to perpetually be a student of this law and investigate continually about it. The more time you give to it, the more contemplation and study, the more you are going to understand it.

Guts & Glory

No Guts, No Glory! That, I was told. One must **G**et **U**sed **T**o **S**neers before you **G**et **U**sed **T**o **S**uccess! It did not make a lot of sense at the start of my journey. Seemed just like those fantastic poetic phrases we can often use without much comprehension. But the fact is, it is true! Over the years, that became much and much clearer as I kept looking for that elusive success with my ego intact. Actually, I came to realize that lack of guts to face your fears can be a great undoing to your mission. There is nothing much worth doing that will not require a great application of guts. Success is not for the fainthearted. It is for those who are daring and willing to go against the grain. If you do what everyone else does, you end up with what everyone else has. I guess you already know what everyone else has. It is exactly what you do not want! Look around and check the majority of people you see in the society. What percentage represent the people who live the kind of life you would like to live? Answer to yourself. I probably do not belong to your locality, but I do guess they are very few people. Now, here is the second question, part of the test. Find out what they have done to be where they are. Were guts involved?

Just in order that I may not assume, in simple terms, guts simply means having a daring attitude to go for what you want without obeying your fears or listening to people who discourage you or sneer at you in any way. You get used to them and move on. You cannot afford to feel ashamed doing what ought to be done! One must have guts in order to succeed. You must have the ability to walk the less traveled paths and daringly explore the new territories. Be warned, no one is going to praise you in this. If you are looking for praise, you will miss it and probably quit. People will congratulate you and sing your song when you are already successful, or at least have tasted some bit of it.

Remembering a few years back when I attended a particular business convention in Cape Town, South Africa, we had the opportunity to be addressed by a great leader called Bill Bins; one of the two gentlemen who brought a Network Marketing company called Golden Products (a NeoLife Company brand) into Africa. He related a story of how they first landed in Africa through South Africa. Bill told us that the moment they chose to come to Africa, the first person to discourage him was his mother. She told him, "Son, why do you want to go to Africa? It is a hostile and very dangerous place. You will die in Africa!" He ended up defying the odds and followed his heart. Deep within him, he believed there is great potential for success and did not have to listen to his mother, however loving and sincere she could be. Golden Company ended up being one of the most well known Multi-level Marketing (MLM) companies in Africa and Australia courtesy of his dream, despite his mother's advice against it. He has become successful many times over and he is Living the Dream! He told us, "When you set out to do something great, people who love you the most will give you the worst advice." It is true!

Bill said, "only two things are necessarily in order to build a great organization; a dream and people who can believe in that dream." This was also true to him because the person who showed him the business was the Founder. He told him that at "one time, this company is going to grow all over the world and millions of people will be changing their lives through it". He believed and became part of the people to drive the vision to its fulfillment. It took a lot of guts to do that. So, my dear friend, have GUTS!

History is filled with people who developed their vision and went for their dreams because of their guts. Take Jonas Salk, the man who came up with polio vaccine. You ever heard of how he was discouraged and sneered, told how useless and fruitless his agenda was? He ultimately made it and is now honored all over the world. Imagine what would have happened had he listened to the naysayers! Be ready to get people who will tell you nothing positive about what you are doing. In selling, we are calling it rejection. Some of your family members will think you are crazy. Even the family of Jesus of Nazareth at one point thought he was crazy and went for him to take him back home! Read Mark 3:21. Your friends will desert you. Your close associates will quit on you. You will look stupid and feel like you are a total let-down to yourself, your family and the rest. A public failure. It is okay. Just do not quit. Do not let someone else determine for you what you can do and what you cannot do. Follow your dream, follow your heart. The reason it is yours is because it is not public and does not need to make sense for others. Do not seek to be popular at this stage. When you succeed, you will be popular anyway. Donald Trump is a classic example! I hope you already know how 'almost' the whole world including poll-stars predicted his failure when he announced he would run for the presidency of the United States. The media was all anti-Trump! Mr. Trump is an example of what it means to have guts!

In my early years of Network Marketing, I was called names! People rebuked and sneered at me countless times. I recall an instance when someone asked me, a former colleague in the last company I worked for as a Network Support Engineer. He said to me; “Paul-Peter, what is wrong with you? You are a whole engineer. Why the hell do you quit your lucrative job to go peddle soap and drugs like a loser! Are you out of your senses?”

What he called drugs were food supplements. The business I started was to distribute detergents and supplements among others. If only I listened to him, and many others like him, I would not be writing this book you are now reading. How did I respond? To most of such remarks, I would only smile and keep silent. I have been mocked and called various names of my products; both in public and private. If you do not have what others call a 'thick skin', you cannot make it. A lot of guts is required here coupled with faith in yourself, your products and your mission. It may not be perfect. You may be wrong, but aim at refining your idea as you go along. But do not be out to please sneers. The best revenge, someone once said, is massive success! Just because they sneer at you, get the fuel to move on and prove them wrong! You can do it!

If you keep on keeping on and start seeing success, hopefully soon but most often after a very long dry spell, the final stage of GUTS becomes **G**etting **U**sed **T**o **S**uccess. Not Sneers anymore! And trust me, You Can Do It! Live Your Dream!

Persistence and Passion
Failure is my teacher
And success, my graduation
Love does not come from above
It comes from determination
Persistence and passion will rebel
Redemption will be mine
I will no longer accept to fail

William McLaughlin (2015)

Chapter 3

DISCIPLINE

Investing in You to Get Better

The formula is Be-Do-Have. Not the other way round like many people think. You become disciplined then you will do the things that disciplined people do. Only then will you be able to achieve the type of results that disciplined people attain. Again, you must become the person you want, in your mind and spirit, then you will do what needs to be done in order to have the corresponding results. If, for example, you want to be successful, it does not start by having the successes. It starts with you. You must go through the discipline of being a successful person in order that you may be someone who does what successful people do; acquiring their habits, so that you can achieve the successes you aspire for.

This did not make sense to me the first time. I would not blame you if you cannot understand it either. Rather, I would congratulate you because you are doing the right thing: finding time to study it in this book. Your thirst for knowledge has brought you to this fountain and you are willing to do your best to absorb everything possible! Your thirst is, hopefully, being quenched. You are in the process of acquiring new understanding, new beliefs, new attitudes and thus growing yourself and becoming the person you want to and can be. You are working on your **T**houghts as you work on your knowledge which will hopefully lead to some deliberate and spontaneous **A**ctions and thus **R**esults. That is the foundation.

> *Discipline is the bridge between goals and accomplishments.*
>
> *---Jim Rohn---*

For a long time, I kept debating in my heart what could be the difference between discipline and obedience and which of the two could be superior. It bothered me which of the two I would choose, if I were to pick one. In the end, my judgment favored discipline. Though I did not fully understand it as I do today, it appealed to me. Discipline, to me, simply meant choosing to do the right thing irrespective of my feelings or anyone's opinion even if it meant a little disobedient. Obedience, on the other hand, meant to me that I am not supposed to question an order issued to me. I simply needed to execute an instruction whether I was in agreement with it or not as long as it came from a source that commanded a higher level of honor. Those were the days I was in year one and two in secondary school. I guess that was not very far from the truth. In other words, it seemed to me that in being obedient, I have to trust the other party's judgment, not mine.

Today, now that I know, I understand where obedience can be applicable and where discipline should be applied. I also understand how important these two things can be. Because my concern for now is discipline, I take this opportunity to give you the definition that has served me very well so far.

> *Discipline is either self-discipline or no discipline at all.*
>
> *---Unknown---*

Discipline is the act of doing what ought to be done, as it ought to be done or even better, whether you feel like doing it or not. That means it is not how you feel in your body that will dictate whether you are going to do it or not. You just do it! The person who carries such acts of discipline is, therefore, referred to as disciplined. When you are disciplined, you do not make judgments based on your moods or feelings. You do not act according to how you feel, the weather, etc. You just do what you had purposed to do, according to your schedule. If it is the right thing to do, you have to do it. And that is the beginning of one of the most important steps in leadership; self-governance. Self-governance, which can also be called self-leadership, comes from self-discipline. It means you obey your own orders and do not break your own rules.

> *A strong man is in charge of his emotions. A weak man is a slave to his emotions.*
>
> *---Otieno Paul-Peter---*

It is often said, and I agree, that discipline means self-discipline or no discipline at all. Once you are disciplined as an individual, once you have self-discipline, it means you are truly and totally disciplined. It means you respect yourself. This is not a public relations thing; it has nothing to do with pleasing others. It has something to do with self-respect. You tell yourself this is what you are going to do and you stick to it. You commit to yourself and become answerable to your own self. You do not do it to look good for others. Most of discipline is not sweet to self. The acts of discipline entail much discomfort and pain. And that is what qualifies the statement...'whether you feel like doing it or not.' It is because it is not very exciting.

Most acts of discipline wage war against the body; against the flesh. Your body feels like ‘I want to sleep’ and your mind/spirit tells you ‘that's not right. You must go and exercise’. And you obey your mind and take control of your body. Your body advises you to hit on the snooze button. Your mind tells you ‘it is time to wake up. You are the one who set this time, chief. Wake up!' Then you choose to wake up. Now, if you continue doing this and you set your mind for this every time, then you are being disciplined.

Sample this. You make a decision that you are going to jog every Monday, Wednesday and Friday morning from 6:00am-6:30am. Now, when that time comes, do not start debating whether or not you should go. That is indiscipline! You have to do it whether you slept late or early, whether you are hungry or full, whatever may have happened. Unless, perhaps, you are really sick. But remember that if you are disciplined, no excuse is acceptable! Again, if you told yourself that you are not going to take any more cakes, then that is it! No cakes! It does not matter if it is your own birthday or if cake is in plenty. If you have decided to read at least one chapter every morning before you eat your breakfast or every evening before you sleep, you must do it.

One day, attending a leadership workshop, a very successful business leader was talking to us. This is someone who earns millions of dollars in a year from his businesses. He was talking about discipline in relation to reading of books. He said that it is his discipline to read one chapter before he sleeps. Here is the interesting part; that even when he is sleepy, he will have to read. He will stand and read on his feet. That some days he can be so sleepy that he finds himself sleeping while on his feet trying to take his daily dose of a chapter a night before retiring to bed, and the book drops from his hands, but he wakes up at the fall of the book only to pick it and continue reading. It is that serious! That is his level of discipline. What is your level? Are you someone who only does what is comfortable and not what is supposed to be done? Answer to yourself.

You may ask, why is this important? And the answer is this: you cannot be two people at the same time. You can only be one person and that is you. If you build a particular habit, it is yours wherever you are, whenever. A human being is a habit-forming creature. Whatever you choose to cultivate is what finally becomes your habit and gets strongly ingrained into your subconscious mind. Your entire being operates, vastly, from the 'data files' and 'program codes' stored in your subconscious mind. It basically forms your operating system much like computers. Everything you read, watch or hear has a possibility of forming part of your operating system; being entrenched into your subconscious mind and thus forming your control mechanism. What I am trying to say is that if you set a precedence of breaking your promises, you become someone who, even involuntarily, breaks promises and thus you somewhat, always, find yourself breaking more and more promises. It becomes a very big hurdle to unlearn that habit and implant another replacement. It is more-or-less like a monkey on your back; difficult to get rid of. That is the way addiction also works. That means if you started exercising on Monday, then on Wednesday you tell yourself, "I am very tired today, let me rest and resume tomorrow", that's the way you fail and thus, implant in you not only the habit of breaking your own rules, orders and disobeying yourself, but also the habit of failure. This is so important a principle in success that no one can circumvent it. It does not matter which profession or career you are in, whether you are an athlete, a musician, factory worker, a farmer, a doctor, name it! The principle is the same. We are all operating under the same universe and thus the same universal laws that respect no man or beast!

> *Habits are formed. Good habits are formed by, first, a firm resolution, then discipline to stick until it becomes comfortable.*
>
> *---Otieno Paul-Peter---*

The same principle of discipline is what will make some people indulge in dishonorable habits. Some people will drink responsibly while others carelessly. Others become like beasts when they think of certain things like sex. They have no control. They can rape a he-goat! This is because they have kept rewarding their impulse/urge for it and thus they become slaves through that act of 'negative loyalty' or simply doing the wrong thing repeatedly enough to implant the irresistible habit of doing it. They become their own slaves; slaves for their flesh. Taking control of every situation and making rational decisions based on your principles and high discipline standards make you a master of yourself and 'captain of your soul'. You take the leadership responsibility and stay in charge. That is true leadership;

following values and principles in spite of feelings or circumstances.

Back in my village, I would see girls always getting babies before they are married; a baby after the other, despite this bringing them a great degree of stress and shame. What kept them doing it again and again? That irresistible impulse! Where does it come from? You find someone who has been really good and straightforward, one day he gives in to a drink or extra-marital affair and that becomes the starting point. It is the first time that it is difficult to do and you feel some powerful force to resist it. The second is easier than the first and the nth time is not only easier but also much more fun, a way of life, a form of civilization. Over time, what initially was unimaginable to you has even become fun and normal. Before one realizes, an unwanted action has become a habit; immorality has become 'moral' because the moral level has been degraded. Do you see where we are coming from? You want to form a habit of success!

In life, you are a leader. Everyone is. The first person to lead is usually yourself. It is through this same self-discipline that you can lead yourself in the right way. Self-discipline is self-leadership. The better you become at leading yourself, the better you could be at leading others. And, you know what, your value goes up according to your leadership level. Therefore, in your self-leadership, you could choose to be guided by your mind or your body, your reasoning or your emotions. I can tell you for sure, your flesh is the worst leader you could follow! It always wants the things your heart is against and keep pushing you towards them. And if you do not take care, you could descend 'below the level of a beast' as James Allen put it in his timeless classic book, *As a Man Thinketh*. Beware!

Taming the Cobra of Negativity

Along the same line, remember that your thoughts, as we have said, control almost everything in your life. You have ever heard, most certainly, about the power of attitude. Numerous books have been written about the subject of Positive Thinking. We talked about it at length in the second chapter. Your negative thoughts, otherwise negative attitude, must be tamed through an act of discipline. There is no remedy for negativity for one who is indisciplined! No one has it, and no one shall provide it. I normally say that working on your attitude is a full time job. It only takes discipline to do this full-time job. You must be disciplined in your thinking. Choosing judiciously to think only what you ought to think and not just anything that comes to your mind. Thinking is such an important work that cannot be left uncontrolled. Discipline is the right tool for this. I guess you are now starting to understand why Being must precede Doing.

The normal functioning of a human mind is that thoughts of all kinds shall come in; negative and positive. You choose which will ultimately be accepted into your control room, that is your subconscious mind. If you choose to, and with practice, you can have a strategy that you immediately summon into operation whenever an unwanted thought crosses your mind. Notice that this also soon becomes your habit and its implementation sort of becomes very natural and automated. That is the same formula to get rid of negative thoughts in your life and start becoming positive. The same way you learn to type or play a piano or drive without much thinking.

> *Affirmation without discipline is the beginning of delusion.*
>
> ---*Jim Rohn*---

The Author of Chicken Soup for the Soul, Mr. Jack Canfield, relates in his book, Success Principles, a story where in their company, they wanted to end negativity. They decided that every-time someone uttered a negative statement, he would be fined a certain amount of money and everyone religiously complied. By the end of a year, the sum would be used for charity. At first, people caught themselves in such situations that warranted fines and much money was collected. But over time, as the mind started relating negativity with debits in their pockets or bank accounts, less and less people were caught and finally there was no element of negativity in the whole company! Discipline is the foundation of it all. Disciplined thinking.

One way you can deal with this is the use of

affirmations; trying to switch your mind immediately you catch yourself dwelling in negative emotions to something positive through affirmations to the contrary. For example, if you started falling into self-pity and dwelling on how miserable you are, upon catching yourself you could start saying aloud "I am blessed! I am happy! I am unique! I am talented...etc" And you can start counting your blessings, achievements and successes. Whatever may make you happy. See it and feel it as you say it. Your mind is soon going to respond and your feelings will follow. Another way is to use your imagination and start thinking of something you love. There are several ways of dealing with this. Whatever works for you, do it. It should be something that uplifts your emotions and makes you feel good. Not negative indulgences as some people would. Just disciplined, positive habits.

Disciplined Focus

Immediately my dad learnt that he was not going to afford my school fees, after having squandered the proceeds from the loan he had secured from a teachers' cooperative society, he sent me to Mombasa. I would go live with his younger brother who was working in one of the many tourist hotels in that town and thus was, allegedly, better off financially. The brother had indicated to me that I can go live with him as I pursue my secondary education and he would pay. He actually paid for my examination enrollment fees for

Standard 8, not because he came at the time for enrollment, but because my dad had not paid yet while we were approaching the exams. The head teacher had just paid mine and was waiting to be refunded.

It was in the month of March when I traveled by train to Mombasa. Hoping for good things and was counting myself lucky to have such a considerate uncle. Besides, I had never been to any town. It would be a great exposure. Because I had done some casual jobs, helping in the farms, I had some little money which I used to buy a tiny used rucksack, from one of my relatives, to carry my scanty clothes and a pair of blue slippers for my shoes. I still had some coins for change. My dad gave me the exact fare for train from Kisumu to Mombasa. It would take two days on the road, traveling at night with a full day stop in Nairobi.

It soon became apparent that there was no money to spare for my school fees. My uncle had lots of commitments including planning for his wife's dowry, building himself a house upcountry and another for his mother. Again, he said, my dad ought to take that responsibility because he did not pay his (my uncle's) school fees despite the fact that he was already employed.

All we could do, with his wife, was to go early in the morning to Kongowea market to sell the pieces of clothes for kids which the wife used to make in the house. At around noon we would come back to the house, prepare lunch, do the laundry, dishes then I would get time to go watch videos in the neighborhoods. Off course I did not have money for video and that meant I could only watch introduction parts which were always free and mostly music rather than action. My aunt, here, was frequently sick and more often than not, I would be the one to do all these work alone from early dawn. After about two months without any communication from my dad, I felt my energy waning. Many friends kept giving me advise; get a ***'kibarua'*** that is, casual work, at a building site and start earning money. Soon you will have your own house and live your life. Others would say, 'ask him to take you for a course.' What that meant is that, besides having passed pretty well in school, and qualifying for secondary school, I should ask for a chance to be taken for some technical training like tailoring, carpentry etc. I chose, instead, to go back home and discuss with my dad, once more, how I can go back to school and pursue my dream. Living in Mombasa was not going to help in any way.

> *Know what you want and keep it to yourself.*
>
> *---Donald J. Trump---*

When I arrived home, I looked stupid! I was a total failure in the court of public opinion! I had let myself down. No one would understand why on earth someone who has had an opportunity to live in a major town, like Mombasa, would choose to go back in the name of looking for school. Why couldn't I take a 'course'! How could I fail to think clearly and see that this was an opportunity of a lifetime, to establish myself and live!

It was at this time that I learnt a great lesson in life; people reason differently! And if you are not firm in your dream, you are going to live someone else's dream! You must stay focused, stubborn and steadfast. It does not matter who is giving you advice. You do not have to do anything someone else tells you to do. Do your things the way you judge right and stay focused. At least, in this way, you would not have to blame anyone even if you do not entirely get everything as you anticipated, and you do not have to regret anything. I stood by my goals and dreams. No one else understood me! And no one wanted to. The other beauty is that I did not share much with anyone. Now I see the advantage of that; "knowing what you want and keeping it to yourself" as Donald Trump put it in one of his books, Trump: How To Get Rich.

Powered by my inner belief that education is the key to the life I wanted to live, despite all the challenges, I was determined to find a way to go to school and finally attain a university education. Not that I had seen anyone around who ever did it. So when I came from Mombasa, since my uncle was unable to take me to school as he had earlier suggested, and finding my dad too ill to be disturbed, I did not have a choice but to stay at home, figuring out my next move.

Just around that time, since I vastly had to keep fending for myself and trying to keep up with the lifestyle I acquired in Mombasa (that of having neat clothes, shoes, toothbrush and toothpaste, shoe polish, petroleum jelly among others), I had to be doing something. At this point, my thinking had expanded a bit and it was clear to me that there must be better ways to make a more reasonable living than just working for people in the farms. Then it happened! News got to me that some Germans were providing scholarships for motor vehicle driving and mechanics. This was happening at a polytechnic located in a town about 24 kilometers away from home. One had to present himself/herself with necessary academic papers for interview.

I prepared myself, got my class 8 result slips and a school leaving certificate. To say the truth, the opportunity excited me because, to me then, it would be great to be a mechanic since that would guarantee a source of income. I would own a garage and become rich! So I established an appropriate day and set out very early in the morning, trekking, to Oyugis; the said town. By around 10:30am I had reached and got into the queue. It was my first ever interview, I believe. After a warm and brief discussion with a certain white lady there, I was awarded a scholarship! They would pay everything and I would live within the polytechnic premises except that I had to raise a portion of the entry fee as a commitment. It was only about Ksh.4,000.00 which was approximately USD66.52 at that time. I could not raise this amount of money. In fact, if I could, that alone would afford me a school fees for one school term.

If you come to look at it, I was getting defocused here and would have lost it! I only realized, a few years later, that even most of the mechanics were really not doing as well as I thought. Stay focused to your courses. I did not realize that motor-vehicle mechanics is not engineering that I had aspired to do. But thanks to GOD for I was not able to pick that option.

> *Successful people maintain a positive focus in life no matter what's happening around them. They stay focused on their past successes rather than their past failures, and on the next action steps they need to take to get them closer to the fulfillment of their goals rather than all the other distractions that life presents to them.*
>
> *---Jack Canfield---*

Even after all these, still people kept distracting me with countless issues. Others kept asking why I could not just accept the reality and forget about the schooling. And when, later, life at home became much worse, after my grandmother also died, when I was struggling to keep alive, others still advised me to go away from home and live with my maternal uncle, where my other brother was. But I new that leaving my home town would be the recipe for terminating my schooling completely. I gave no comment; accepting or objecting. Always trying to appear respectful and obedient. It helps, I think.

You must be disciplined in your focus. You must not have a wavering focus that is subject to the wind. That is the relatives, the friends and the likes who would always want to have a say. Focus is a very crucial attribute and many authors have labored to explain what it means. This problem make people jump from this trade to that without learning anything and becoming their best and thus a lot of people sabotaging their own success for the mere lack of focus.

In your journey to the top, you are going to meet countless distraction agents. That is the way life is! If your focus is weak, you can be sure of remaining average at best. Many good opportunities will come along your way and would seduce you away from what you originally set out to do; which is bigger and most important. To me, I had not few. The polytechnic scholarship, Mombasa life, fishing was there (and many people were living on the same). My business was another that could have put me off school line. Because I later started a business that thrived too. But my disciplined focus to the ultimate goal, I would say, rescued me. I pray you maintain your radar in perspective.

Health, Fitness, Exercise

For you to Live Your Dream, you have got to be alive to start with. You have to be there; available in this life. And for you to be there, you must be having your health with you; at least health of the body. Whether poor or otherwise. We are talking about Living Your Dream in this present life and not in the life after. One of the most essential requirements for people who would live their dreams is health; optimal health. I like talking of optimal health as opposed to just health. You could be healthy just because you are not sick, but you are not in optimal health. Optimal health shall include total well-being. Feeling and looking healthy. And you should indeed be healthy. At times you may feel and look healthy while you are not really healthy. I'm told that conditions like cancer or diabetes can reside in you for quite some time before you realize it. But one day you get the disgusting news and shortly after, your life totally changes!

It is also good to know that one who is overweight is not enjoying optimal health. Being underweight is not good either. Equally, one who is under the fear of heart attack, or is under the scourge of chronic lifestyle conditions has not much joy in life. You can not claim to be in optimal health if your entire life is pegged on continuous medication or if you are always on the doctor's strict diet of 'DON'TS'. "Don't eat sugar, don't eat salt, don't drink alcohol, don't, don't…" That is not the health you will enjoy. Is it?

Without your health you have no life. And this is irrespective of whom you are; king or slave, saint or sinner. Health, even in the dictionaries, comes before wealth. It has been said that some people ruthlessly squander their health looking for wealth then quickly spend their entire wealth to regain their (most crucial) health; and most of the times in vain. This is because once health has deteriorated to a breaking-point, it becomes virtually impossible to reverse it to its original status. It is more-or-less like a lady who has given birth to a baby, she cannot become a virgin again. She only has to cope with the new lifestyle. And many meet this situation in their fifties onwards. You do not have to be like them. The good news about this is that it is a matter of choice! Once you resolve to live a healthy lifestyle, the rest is pretty easy. Making firm decisions is a challenge which leaders meet day and night. And that is what the world uses to judge them; their firmness in the resolve to stick to their decisions and fruits therefrom.

> *One quarter of what you eat keeps you alive. The other three quarters keep your doctor alive.*
>
> *---Egyptian Proverb---*

It takes the same old discipline to be in optimal health, that allows you to Live Your Dream! Your health shall be largely determined by your lifestyle. What do you eat? Remember, you are what you eat. There are many people who do not want to take charge of their health. They leave everything to a doctor. They want the (family) doctor to take care of their own health. This is, in my view, a clear recipe for trouble. The fact that you can afford medication does not mean you become reckless with your life and abdicate all the health responsibilities for your life to another person. It is the epitome of irresponsibility. It is like one getting into fire simply because he can afford hospital bills. Besides, remember poor health does not only cost money, it costs you comfort, peace of mind and ultimately, it costs you life. Or should I say, your life, which is the last payment you can give! Your own life. It matters less who you are; whether a carpenter or a preacher, a doctor or a magician. Everyone needs optimal health.

What many people do not realize is that to the hospital or the doctors, you are a customer and thus they (more so in the private sector) would always be happy to have you around. This is a strange friendship; where the hyena is a friend to the antelope. But few realize this. You want to try as much as you can to avoid unnecessary medications or hospital visits. You want to only visit a health clinic for your own (regular) checkup, in order to confirm that you are healthy; preferably only once a year. Perhaps the other reason to take you to a doctor would be to say hello, as a friend, and catch up. This you can do elsewhere; perhaps at a golf club, cinema, school board meeting, among other places. This you can only do by staying healthy. And there is a lot you can do to realize this. I can guarantee you that the doctor will still not go hungry because there will always be enough people to take care of. I mean enough sick people. If you doubt this, just recall the last time you visited a doctor's clinic. Didn't you have to wait? If ‘YES’, then let the other guys continue as you back off because you are now more health-conscious. Besides, more medicine in your body means more toxins in your body.

I have a number of friends in the pharmaceutical industry. Many of them work as medical representatives; selling drugs to doctors and hospitals. So far, two have confided in me about what happens in that industry. And they do not know each other. Neither do they work for the same employer. One told me that he sells but he would not want to swallow those drugs because "*they are just poisons. Even the owners and manufacturers do not want to swallow them so why should I*?" He prefers preventing and avoiding diseases than treating. And when he falls sick, he prefers using a nutritional approach. We are going to discuss this shortly. The other friend also told me, "*you know it is a hard job I do but I have to do it. I sell poisons. I have to convince people to buy these poisons. Remember these are just poisons only that they do not kill instantly when used appropriately. But that is what I have to sell and my team has to do the same; sell poisons.*"

There is this documentary I once watched. It was downloaded and put in a DVD. The DVD was named Food Matters. If you get to YouTube and search for this, you will certainly get some fragments of the same. From this you may be able to learn that pharmaceutical industry may not be as clean and sincere as you may want to think. And I'm saying this not to discredit them. The science of medicine has contributed immensely to the growth and development of mankind. But the appetite for money, in some quarters, has infiltrated it and there is a lot of rot in there; perhaps coupled with a wee bit of ignorance. Do your own objective research and evaluate for yourself. But in the mean time, as much as you can, stay healthy, steer away from pharmaceutical products unless you really have to. How will you do this?

It starts by asking for a second opinion. Do not just trust the opinion of one doctor. Get the habit seeking several views from different practitioners. You will be amazed! Of the recorded causes of death, wrong diagnosis/medication and side effects is actually one of the leading. A friend of mine recently almost knocked off all her teeth if only she heeded the opinion of the first doctor who made an emergency out of the situation until other varied opinions cooled the temper. Just to tell you that not everyone who is diagnosing your condition has all your interests at heart. Still there are enough good doctors and even some more crafty money maniacs. Be careful. You have to be careful with your health to Live Your Dream!

A 500BC Greek, medical genius, Hippocrate of Kos, said, “Let thy food be thy medicine and thy medicine be thy food”. His insight was profound. He was right. More so in the today's world of fast everything; fast food, fast cars, fast Internet, fast cash, et cetera. This is a scientific truth and cannot be mutilated. A human body generates self-defense from the foods he/she ingests. This is true for all living things; animals and plants. That is the reason trees hardly need medication. At least in our village, I know this for a fact. Perhaps in your area you dress wounds for your trees when they get cut lest they die of some infections. Not so at our place. Even wild beasts live full life without any medical interventions. They, somewhat, get healed naturally. How do you explain this? I think GOD, the Creator, Himself did not expect people to have health challenges if they lived well. Just like beasts. Hardly do they get sick. But the only animal with all the health challenges is man; together with a few domestic animals that he takes care of. And yet man is the most knowledgeable of them all! Why is that!

> *It is senseless to trade years of quality health for a few seconds or minutes of excitement.*
>
> *---Otieno Paul-Peter---*

My thinking is that, because man is the cleverest, he should be able to even keep much healthier. Don't you think so? Man can read, learn, research, study, think, figure out. So, compared to other animals, man should be able to tame disease and get rid of it. Man should be able to prevent it and conquer it. But this is not a common sense issue. It is a grim reality. Man gets sick often and dies younger in most cases. You are what you eat!

Take charge of your health, start reading about nutrition. That is the best way to start. Doctors are not Angels. They also make mistakes, and very serious mistakes for that matter, more so in matters to do with how you should eat. It is not a medical school course. Actually it is a new development. So do your own due diligence and give your body what it requires, not what is sweet for the tongue. As I have often said, I learnt that your tongue will always complain about the right foods and be happy with the ones that are bad for your body. But if you continuously give it what is right, soon it will start appreciating them and hate the wrong ones. The same things will happen with your mind and emotions. It is a matter of strict training and discipline. Over time you get to overcome the urge to indulge in wrong things and avoid unnecessary foodstuffs that add no value to you. By the way, that includes smoking and drinking alcoholic drinks; they add no good, just bad to your 'holy' body. When one smokes, it is like he is taking poison and waiting for the consequences, which shall surely come, only that he experiences short joys at the expense of long term health challenges, pains and losses. Do not eat what will kill you if you want to Live Your Dream! Living Your Dream starts with living a healthy lifestyle. Everything in moderation!

You need, as well, to check on your exercises. The nutrition lessons will take you through. It is never as hard as you may want to imagine. It is all in the FEAR element which you will learn more about in this book. It is in your mind. Your mind may make scenes look quite ugly while in reality they are not. So, while studying nutrition as part of your homework, remember to take more fresh fruits and vegetables, more whole grains, minimal fats and sugars, minimal starch and refined foods, more of natural, home grown foods. But be conscious about your health and nutrition. It takes a lot of discipline. Tongue discipline, you may call it. Again, better the pain of discipline than the pain of regret.

Disciplined Activities;

There is a book by Dr. D. Wattle's called The Science of Getting Rich. When it comes to this topic of activities, I remember once reading in that book that getting rich is not a matter of brilliance, location, type of business one is involved in, economy, government of the day, or anything. He says that it is a matter of *DOING things* in a *Certain Way*. Things must be done in a Certain Way to achieve Certain results. It therefore follows that haphazard activities can't achieve any greatness! If you really want to be a success and to Live Your Dream, you must, first of all, show your commitment. This is best demonstrated in your level of discipline in terms of activities. A disciplined program of activities. Remember that part of what determines how your life turns to be is what you do. It is what you do and HOW you do it. You could be doing the right thing but wrongly. Perhaps due to your knowledge or skill level, attitude or out of sheer laziness. If you are pulling when you are supposed to push (the door open), you are doing the right thing wrongly. For whatever reason.

People who want to achieve greatness have a way of doing their work. They always, some how, keep a predictable schedule. If it is a matter of reading a page every day, they will be disciplined enough to do exactly that. In fact, they will miss a meal but not their doze of reading. If it is a matter of exercise, they will do it religiously as if all their lives depended on that. At exactly the predetermined time and nothing will stop them. If they choose to be on a particular diet, they shall always keep it. If it is a matter of continuous improvement of customer experience, they will do it. They will never choose to do anything halfheartedly just because they are tired or something. NO! What has to be done has to be done in the manner in which it is supposed to be done. They do not accept excuses.

At one point one of my early mentors taught me, "….even if you found an excuse dropped down somewhere, do not pick it! Never accept an excuse from anyone and never give it either. In the journey for success, no excuse is good enough...and if you pick it, you are going to be tempted to give it to someone else. So do not pick it!" I still hold this statement in my heart. It makes me look a little too stiff a person to deal with, but that is okay by me. Just like in keeping time. I accept no excuses. I equally give none. And whether others violate this principle or not, it does not affect my sense of value for time. Whenever I get late for anything, it is because I chose to. Or because I allowed it. And, by the way, time keeping is one of the best ways to gauge your level of discipline.

Another great teacher, T. Harv Eker, puts it this way, "No ifs, no buts, no may bes and quitting is not an option!" For this reason, many poor or average people find it difficult to live with or relate with successful people. They find them too strict for them and thus not very accommodative. It is normally because they will not allow excuses. If you agree to meet at a particular place at some time, you must keep that time. They have a culture of keeping timely schedules of activities. To some, this is too rigid and denies them the freedom. But the reality is, such a disciplined way of doing things makes your life more organized, wins you respect from others and increases your value in the market place; setting you apart from the crowd. This is an essential ingredient in the *Being* of a Successful person.

Doing things in a Certain Way! How about spending money? Yes! That too! Personal Money Management is a course I have fallen in love with. I have made money. For some reason, from the time I learnt about money in primary six, making money has been, in many cases, pretty fun. In fact, the art of making money seemed to be running in my DNA. I had thought of becoming financially free when in primary school. I did not know it by that name, but I had that idea and desire already! But this could not happen! Why? Because of lack of knowledge. I had not learnt money discipline; how to take care of the money I earn. Instead, like many people, I kept thinking that it is my income that is little. It is my income which is not sufficient. Much as I had learnt that 'human needs are insatiable', that did not make a lot of sense for me as far as money management is concerned. I know quite many people who are like that. They are wrong! I was wrong. It is my activities involving finances that were indisciplined and thus could not yield admirable results. I was not doing things in the ***Certain Way***. I was indisciplined. Much of this will form a story for another day. But what you need to know in this sub topic is that indisciplined money habit will not yield the results you want.

> *Money in your hands is like having a hare in the bush or fish in the water. You must find away to make it stick to you and benefit you before it breaks away.*
>
> *---Otieno Paul-Peter---*

In brief, because this is not a financial management book, this is what you need to know. Plan with your money. It is not about what you earn. It is what you do with what you earn. The following principles would guide you. Further to these, I recommend you read more about money and money management.

1:There are two types of income; passive and active. Passive income comes from your assets. From your investments. The other comes from your sweat. You really want to grow your passive income.

2:Do your best to always increase your capacity to

earn. This means you work on earning more and more. It does not come by asking for a raise from your employer. It comes by increasing your value in the market place; personal development.

> *Between you and your money, one is a master and the other a slave. Who are you?*
>
> *---Otieno Paul-Peter---*

3:Have a plan of what to do with money before you receive it. Set goals; goals that lead to building your passive income. Remember what we discussed in chapter one?

4:Put aside a portion of your income and invest it. Start small and reinvest back again and again. Do not be complicated with investment. Read books, ask experienced people, attend lectures on the same.

5:Do not wait to start earning enough. It will never happen. Put aside your portion then spend what is left. Not the other way round. Keep at least 10% of your income.

6:Sub-divide your income accordingly for various purposes, but do not live on more than 70% of your total income. That is, if you would want to be financially free at some point in time. Financial freedom means, you can live, exclusively, on your passive income, the lifestyle of your choice, and your earning is neither pegged on your presence nor on your current activity.

Personal Development Regimen

It is said that nothing gets better unless you get better. Nothing changes unless you change. There is no known way that is as direct and doable as continuously growing yourself when it comes to success. It is a known fact that the only reliable and sustainable way to earn more is to increase your capacity to earn. Many people normally have this problem of "I don't save because I do not earn enough." The sure answer to the problem is to increase your market value and also become better at managing your personal finances.

Every skill is learnable and if someone else has done it, you too can do it. We do not mean to say it is easy. It is never easy and, I believe, it should not be. No one achieves success with hands in the pocket. If it were easy, majority of the population would be really successful and really happy. But you and I know pretty well that just the opposite is the case; very few people are rich, and even fewer happy people. It is hard! Getting rich, having enough money for your needs and for play, is hard. Really hard! It requires hard, focused and consistent work. But still no guarantees. Then what does that mean to you and me?

If we cannot get anything that we want, it is most probably because we do not know how to get it. That is it! It does not matter how many people ever got it. What matters is whether we really want it and whether we are willing to commit to getting it, *whatever it takes*; learning new ideas, skills or languages. We can learn how to get that which we want then go get it. If we want to fly an aircraft, we shall go to flying school. If we want to earn more money, we have to learn how to earn more. If we want a particular lifestyle, it is a subject of knowledge. Adding more hours into our labor does little improvement in our earnings at best. It is the value we put in; not the hours. And you do not have to rely on history here. Remember that almost all the inventors in history did not rely on any history to back up their endeavor. The Wright brothers had never seen anyone flying a plane in order to conceive the idea of building one. Mr. Graham Bell had never seen one with a telephone, John D. Rockefeller had never seen kerosene as much, Thomas Edison had not seen light powered by Electricity and the list is endless. All these came into being due to their vision and conviction that it is possible and their unceasing appetite for knowledge and the discipline to keep their focus on what is most important to them and to be disciplined in their own personal development in order to be the right people who could obtain the objects of their desire.

> *All personal growth can be summed up into leadership development. The more you grow the more influential you become.*
>
> *---Otieno Paul-Peter---*

Here is the point, you must be disciplined to keep

growing, be disciplined enough to keep on acquiring new skills and incessantly improving your skills. It takes disciplined effort. Some of the very fundamental skills necessary for your success include communication, emotional intelligence, interpersonal relationships, teamwork, selling, financial management among others. In general, your leadership level must go high. Get this right: No meaningful success is attained by solos. Success is a teamwork venture and thus your leadership must be good enough to have people willing to follow (and work with) you. That means that, at some point in life, the only important subject you want to keep learning more and more is leadership; improving your ability to lead. And, as I normally say, this means your ability to sell; selling yourself, your ideas, mission among others. If you still hate that word, you are reading a wrong book. You are not going to Live Your Dream! But before you drop the book, let me share with you something.

Before I really chose to become a full-time entrepreneur, I did not know much about selling. My attitude towards selling was very poor and limiting. I kept looking at myself as an engineer and that meant, on my side, no need to know how to sell, let alone to attempt. How naive I was! My thinking was not conforming to my desires, I would say. My desire to ultimately Live large and achieve financial freedom in large scale could not conform to my poor attitude about selling. I soon realized, through watching and hearing almost every motivational speaker talk, that I could not do without the skill of selling. In fact, as I have said somewhere, my Network Marketing business was doing badly. No one was buying my products. The products were great! Very effective and sellable. No one was joining my business either! And that kept me worried. Almost always thinking I made a mistake starting this venture. I kept trying to figure out what was not right. The thought would consume me and make me feel desperate. Feeling that the people who told me "this thing doesn't work" were really right!

> *What we fear most to do is usually what we most need to do.*
>
> *---Ralph W. Emerson---*

One day I took time, being a scientist, to do a survey around and identify if my problem was across the board or it was an isolated case. I can promise you that I did not have to use my T-square, Poison or Fisher Distribution learnt in the school of Mathematics in the university in order to see that I was just one of the few whose products were, though using the same price list in the same market, a little too costly for anyone to buy and the business too hard for people to do. At one point I was wondering if I were actually the last person to get started in this business because that would mean that there were no people left to join me. And so, as usual, I was determined to do my own introspection and unscientifically research on this business.

My appetite for knowledge heightened. It became obvious that there is something I did not know, and that was my liability. If others were successfully doing it, I could do it too! Same market, same price list, same products, same warehouse? Others, some of whom are not as educated, do not look as smart and are not as connected, are able to do it and succeed massively, surely something was wrong with (the person in) me. I kept pondering and meditating. Attending talks and trainings.

One evening I got an epiphany. Attending the usual trainings, I listened to a leader speaking and one of the statements that struck me was, "..one cannot have the same problem every time. That is silly. You must learn how to solve it! How can a problem keep recurring to you every other time and you are not doing anything about it? Not even reading or asking. Why not even register for a course related to that problem in order to look for a solution?" I felt the talk was directed to me and after a thorough evaluation, I chose to face reality. As Trump says, the mother of all advice that he got form his mother, "Trust in God, but be true to yourself." I remembered during my days training people computer skills. In many instances a student would claim something is not working; perhaps a mouse, a keyboard or even an application in the computer. And I remember asking them that direct and penetrating question; "why is it not working for you and yet it works for others?" I would then follow by the statement; "I know where the problem is; it is in between the desk and the computer." And more often than not, that was the case. The student was the problem; lack of knowledge. This time round, I was the problem and I had to face the reality or perish. I had to choose to grow if I was serious about my goals.

My growth from a poor salesperson to a professional one is what we can call personal growth. It means you are growing in knowledge and abilities. In skills and influence. When one pursuing his/her dream is faced with circumstances like mine, where things do not seem to work and hope appears to be diminishing, then it is clear that something is lacking. That is the time to re-evaluate the degree of commitment to the goals. That is why, if someone has no compelling reason to succeed, he/she hardly succeeds. No fuel to propel you beyond your comfort zone. At least I had compelling reasons. I started out on my quest for the knowledge and skill of selling. And I started with a goal to become one of the top sellers and have fun doing it! I remembered how hard physics was at the university and how frustrating mathematics was. I told myself, 'if I could do that, this too I can do.' Your past successes can be a very important reservoir of consolation and energy to keep on keeping on. Use them as much as possible.

> *Leadership and learning are indispensable to each other.*
>
> *---John F. Kennedyr---*

In your endeavor to acquire new skills, you really do not have to believe everything you read or everything someone tells you. That is a very important statement. Sometimes what works for someone else will not necessarily work for you. Remember that learning is about drawing your own conclusions after you have read what you were supposed to read and after experimenting your own way. One must make judgment from information gathered and, where possible, as much as possible, test the results against the hypothesis. That is how you become a good student and could grow to be better than your teachers. You read widely and extensively then let your conclusion be a subject of your own analysis and tests. That is how I arrived at the fact that the skill of selling is a central skill no entrepreneur can do without. Great entrepreneurs on earth have it and boast about it. I was determined to be an entrepreneur just like them. And I realized that all great entrepreneurs are leaders. Thus leadership is closely related to entrepreneurship and selling. My desire for success pushed me to do the extra-ordinary. I not only learnt to sell and improve my businesses, but also I started training my own distributors, partners and associates on how to sell. My leadership level grew and my business grew proportionately. Life became fun! Naturally, I love teaching and enjoy teaching my own material; what I have learnt on my own or discovered through experience and experiments.

Up to now, I have talked to countless number of people

about these topics, professionally and otherwise. Personal development became one of my pet subjects. No one believes, today, that I was once an amateur in this field! That is what I call personal growth! I improved my ability to earn! I learnt to sell, to take care of my customers and keep them, to build and handle teams, to motivate my business associates to grow and achieve more and my business had to grow in proportion to my personal growth just as yours will.

I read and study every single day. I read, again in the words of Donald J. Trump, "..as much as I can, but not as much as I want." The first and the last thing I do every day is to read something. I am always thirsty for more. And all successful people behave that same way. You better start doing it if you are yet to. Notice that success is not a destination to be reached but a lifestyle. One of my all-time favorite speakers, Jim Rohn, once said, "you better miss a meal but never miss your 30 minutes of daily reading. Just 30 minutes a day." Les Brown, on the other hand, recommends one hour a day. Then he says that because his dreams are bigger, he does more than an hour. It did not take long before I could realize that the time you take to read and study something in your field is not lost! And as a leader or an entrepreneur, you will need to read widely because, to an extent, you are a generalist. That time is the time you take to sharpen your axe in order to be able to cut the trees that block the way to Living Your Dream!

Many people have excuses for not reading. They keep

looking for long explanations why it is not possible for them with their crazy schedules, young babies, cows making noise, the traffic jam, neighbors always quarreling and all sorts of justifications. I agree with them. It may not be that easy; more so if there is not instant reward. But somebody once said, *"you will always get time to do what is important for you."* My remedy for such people is this, for I know for sure that they are not reading this book, but should you find them, here is what you need to tell them, if they are really, really, sure they want to live a happy, successful and significant life, then they have no choice and the earlier they could start reading the better. Here is where their reading time is: one is on the road when going to or coming from work. If you are not driving, you can read. If you are driving, you can listen to an audio book. Instead of listening to radio talks or any such stuff that does contribute not much positive to your future, engage your mind and read. Reading, by the way, is also the only way to exercise your brain/mind and to ignite ideas to flush out as insights. It is through reading that some wonderful ideas will find an opportunity to approach you like a vision. You will get the energy and the drive to go for what you want. And there are audio books to listen to as you work on something; perhaps driving or washing your dishes. To me, holding a book in my hands and reading works much

> *Education liberates.*
>
> *---My teacher, Philip Olela---*

better. I am a slow reader and take time to grasp ideas. So listening to audio can force me to a speed I am not comfortable with. But I do listen to stuff when doing other things. It is great!

I remember that in secondary school, for those few occasions I had to be in school, I did not have a place to read from other than in class. Many are the days I could not say with certainty where I would spend my night or get my next meal. Even for the times I had a place to go to, no one guaranteed me paraffin, which I needed so badly, in order to oil my little tin lamp so I could have a chance to read from home. So what did I do? Simple; I read on my way to school. I read on my way from school too. Notice that I was neither driving nor commuting as a passenger in a cab/bus. And that is not to mean someone was driving me as I take my seat on the back left either. I was walking to school and would read on my way as I walk. But the school was not far from home; just about two kilometers away. For some reason, other than the times I would take to read when in class, noticing that I could not do it at home, I was still among the top students in my class. That is a miracle! But I think the main reason was the degree of passion I had for schooling and the clear goals I had. But to many, that is simply luck or a miracle. What is driving you?

> *You can't climb the ladder of success with your hands in the pocket.*
>
> *---Unknown---*

What are your reasons?

My upline director, in my network marketing business, used to tell us this: "you cannot be too busy to re-fuel your car". I agree. I guess you agree as well. To us, re-fueling meant attending the regular team trainings and talks or sitting one-on-one with your leader/coach to learn something. These trainings provided fuel to keep us going. They formed points of insight. Points of personal growth. To say the truth, those were the days I learnt about the term '*personal development*' and '*personal growth*'.

I know I am preaching to the converted, but it is not in vain. You shall use it to teach your people. You are already a reader. Else you would not be reading this page now. So kindly allow me to share this.

Being too busy to read is an equivalent of being too busy to eat. Food is for the stomach, reading is food for the mind. Brain also gets emaciated! Thou shalt have to be a reader! What is likely to happen if you do not get time to re-fuel your car? That is exactly what will happen in the journey to your dream if you do not want to create time to read. Today, technology has made things much simpler. You can use ear-phones even as you walk in order to build your mind and enlarge your knowledge base. You can record lessons. You can read on your phone directly from the Internet. All you need to do is have a clear and deliberate reading program. Inculcate, into your system, a reading culture. It is an attitude issue. Become a reader in order to be a leader. And notice that if you want to be a success then you definitely want to be a leader and that means you want to be a reader. I cannot over emphasize this. Choose for yourself, as Joshua told the Israelites, what will be suitable for the life you want. As for me, because my dreams are bigger and keep growing, personal growth is not a choice and up to now, I have a daily time table of what to read. Besides that, I take time to read at every opportunity; whether waiting to be served in the banking hall, waiting for a cab, at the airport or waiting for someone. Any waiting time is a reading time.

> *We all must suffer from one of the two pains; either the pain of discipline, which weighs grams, or the pain of regret, which weighs tons.*
>
> *---Jim Rohn---*

For any new habit you want to form, like these habits of discipline, just know that they will take you between three to four weeks if you keep doing them daily without interruption, and henceforth they become your habits. A new habit takes approximately 21-30 days to be fully installed into your system. This is true even in the cases of addiction, with some modifications which we shall not cover in this book.

Education

Learning is so-critical, knowledge is the key
To unlock the doors of the universe for me
It's importance is unparalleled,
Constant assimilation - so vital
My ultimate goal is to never let my mind be idle
In a world full of mediocrity,
I utilize my curiosity
Mental stagnation leads to cranial vegetation
Education is my tool for discovery
That leads me to enlightened mastery.

-----Jeff Holloway--------

Chapter 4

DISAPPOINTMENT

A Way of Life

If there is one thing you will have to contend with in your journey to Living Your Dream, it is this ugly animal called Disappointment! Armed with the first 3Ds; your first 'D' being the Dream, which is actually your Destination(if you wish) or the "predetermined worthy ideal", your second 'D' which is Determination backed by a burning Desire and the third 'D' which is Discipline, you should not find it hard at all to Disappoint your Disappointments. It is a Discipline too! Disappointing your Disappointments, that is. Disappointments, I say it again, are part of life, and that is the way you should treat them. This is why many people talk about developing a 'thick skin' in your pursuit to success. That means you refuse to be worn out. You cannot let go, you cannot quit! In other words, quitting is not an option. You started and thus you must finish. Successful people do not know the meaning of quitting.

> *Every problem is a gift. Without problems we wouldn't grow.*
>
> *---Anthony Robins---*

Disappointments will test your degree of resilience and focus, your level of determination and discipline, the strength of your desire and belief. You will be stretched beyond the elastic limits and more. That is growth! You will feel pain, feel like a failure, and you will certainly feel stupid. Nothing will make sense, and, in many instances, quitting will seem very palatable and most welcome. This is the time of following the blind faith! No evidence except, perhaps, in the mind. But you must pass the test! You must pass this level before you see the success you are looking for. It is, actually, an indicator that you are on the right track. As I am told, a wise guy once said, *"you always know when you are on the path to success. It is uphill all the way."* You will certainly realize that this agrees with some of the wise statements you might have heard before like *"it is darkest at dawn"* and the rest. And in our culture, we have a saying that *"a boat capsizes toward the shores"*, which means it is when the destination is near that people give up, that failure overtakes well-meaning people who are following their dreams.

When I had set to achieve a director level in my Network Marketing (NWM) business, this was (and still is) a very prestigious level in the company, my mentor told me the following: "remember that your enemy, the devil, is not happy with your resolution, with your success. You are going to meet the greatest hurdles ever in this business. You are going to be tested before you are trusted. It is when your success is near that the devil fights the hardest and fiercest. Stay alert and focus on winning." I understand that better today.

> *Ask not for less problems. Instead, ask for more skills. Ask not for less burden. Instead, ask for a stronger back.*
>
> *---Jim Rohn---*

The reason I must tell you this is not to discourage you, but to encourage you. It is because I do not want you to quit. I want you to eventually Live Your Dream! To be forewarned is to be forearmed, I am told. I used to get excited to be told of the problems I am going to meet on the way because that prepared me beforehand and thus I did not have to be surprised; though some tests along my way seemed to be endless! Indeed some of your problems are going to appear to be endless too. But every time I would meet these difficulties, I would be assured that I am on the right track. So should you. People get excited when they get assurance that they have not lost the direction to their destination. On the path to success, the road signs are usually the troubles you meet. Without them, you better be sure you are not doing the right thing and thus cannot expect to get the right result.

Winning Formula

Every pursuit has a big toll to pay and everyone, at one point or the other, has felt like quitting. My first experience, off-course, was when I was looking for school fees to join secondary school. I had to take just more than year outside before finally joining a school to start my secondary education; a critical pre-qualification to university education. Again it happened when I was supposed to be in year three but had to leave and go look for fees. It was not easy. My benefactor, the deputy head teacher then, had just been transferred and thus I did not have anyone to reason out my case. That was the time many people advised me to quit and concentrate on what can get me income so I can start my life; taking care of my siblings. I took, again, over one year outside school before 'miraculously' finding my way back to class for just less than ten months before sitting for the final exams. Many times I almost let go but the dream inside me would not let me. I knew all my future was pegged on my education. Actually, there are people who still doubt if I surely did the final exams. They cannot explain how I went to college! Some, still, have no idea that I ever went back to school and even college. The only thing they know about me is that I dropped off school.

Later after being in employment for over three years, I joined the big business of Network Marketing, which really came to me at the best time. It did not take long before I started feeling that I had done a mistake. My goal was to be financially free and to keep myself and family in optimal health. It was clear to me that the job I was doing was not going to guarantee these things while these had been my dreams all along from childhood. I could see already people who were following this business path and were doing much better, or at least seemed so; living the kind of life I wanted to live.

So when I started my business with enthusiasm and was for once, able to visualize where I was headed, I hit a snag! Things were not happening as I had expected. People were quitting on me; some of the distributors I managed to sponsor into the business did not last, others took off the same day they started. I never saw them again. Some of them, even after talking big and promising great time ahead in business, still vanished in thin air. I kept wondering what others were seeing that I was not able to see. I almost quit. It is at this point that a friend handed me a book by Robert Kiyosaki entitled Rich Dad's Cash Flow Quadrant. It was the rescuer, the reason I am still living my dream. After I read his first chapter, 'Why Can't You Get A Job?', I understood better the path I had taken. It was not the path for the majority, but for the minority. I remember how he narrated his story and explained the emotions, values at the core in the four different quadrants. How he almost quit and went to make a call to his rich dad to inform him of the new resolution. And what did rich dad tell him?

"*You can always quit. So why now?*", was his reply.

That was the answer. It took me a couple of weeks trying to digest the message. Which was shortly followed by "***You will Win if you don't Quit.***" Later I understood the meaning. There are always opportunities ahead to quit. So you do not have to quit at this point. Just remember this every time you think like throwing the towel. Kiyosaki says what his rich dad reminded him. The reason he got started. "*Remember why you started*", he said. So, if you've been contemplating quitting, are you quitting because you have a better way or you have achieved your goals? No! So, keep on keeping on. You will win, if you do not quit!

> *You will win if you don't quit!*
>
> *---Rich Dad---*

Not everyone necessarily meets the disappointments. Some are a little lucky not to meet many of them. And perhaps you could be among the lucky few. Others also only experience a moderate level of disappointment. But if you are like some of us, starting with nothing; no one million dollar, no big name, no inheritance and, off-course, not in a first world country, you may be a little as unlucky as many of us. But you can still make it. So, just in case you are yet to meet your fair share of disappointments and you are currently wondering where the heck could they be coming from, I'll take a short-while to explain a few sources. These will enlighten you a little bit and give you some degree of resilience when they actually occur.

So, where do they come from? You may ask!

Your own people will disappoint you

I know this better. When I was unable to go to school, I thought some relatives would help pay my school fees. In fact, many of them showed an indication they were going to assist. An uncle of mine who was working in Mombasa, the one who actually paid my enrollment fee for Primary School Certificate examinations, assuredly told me to go study in Mombasa and live with him there. That he would take care of my secondary schooling. He did not. In fact after all that struggle to reach Mombasa, I was disappointed beyond my imagination. How naive I was! To start with, he did not even bother to come pick me from the railway station. Remember there were no mobile phones then and, off-course, it was my first time to reach Mombasa, a large old town about 900km from home. I was just about 15 years old. I did not have any other person I knew in Mombasa and, also, no money in my pocket at all. How I finally got to his place is a story for another day. And what was he doing, in stead of getting worried about this little village boy, being that train time had long elapsed? You are right! He was reading his newspaper in his house, stretching his leg across the table waiting to partake of lunch and go to work! You already know he did not pay and so I had to go back home after two long months of waiting, to keep seeking alternative solutions.

When I eventually started school a year later, and was mostly out due to fees problem, another 'serious' uncle of mine came and told me, *"when they send you away again for lack of school fees, just come to me. I will take care of it."* He was a board member in the same school. It did not take long. I did as he said and what did he tell me? Yes! Instead of asking how much it was and writing a cheque, a promissory note or a letter to the school pledging to do something, he said *"now go tell your father. He must take responsibility. He cannot just keep to his bottle when you are out of school. Look for him!"*

At a certain point I was to go revise my courses before the university intake. I talked to my close relatives who lived in Nairobi, quite a distant from home. About 400Km away; a capital city in Kenya, it is a fairly large city where anyone can get lost if not properly guided; at least on the first visit. It is actually the largest city in East and Central Africa. There were no Google maps then. I had to go to The University of Nairobi, where the Joint Admission Board (JAB) sat; the agency that recruited university students for the public universities in Kenya at that time. I had not been to Nairobi and knew no one, no estate, no direction. After a thoughtful consideration, I knew it would not be easy to go and come back the same day. I knew it would be possible to get lost in the city or meet some wrong characters who would endanger my life. I considered this guy a gentleman, at least based on what I could see, and fairly successful. So I approached him and asked if I could seek shelter for a night or two at his residence in Nairobi when I go to revise my degree courses. To me, that was a simple thing and he had a choice of telling me no and it would be fine with me. He was a jovial guy and readily said YES! He willingly shared his cellphone number with me, urging me to call him immediately I reach the city. I was excited. It was just during the advent of mobile phones and even owning one was a sign of prestige. We had a deal. I would travel during the night and arrive in the morning, by bus, and give him a call to come pick me so I could be guided on my way to the University for my assignment.

> *No matter the size of your disappointment, you still have freedom over your attitude.*
>
> *---Otieno Paul-Peter---*

The day came and I started my journey. The reason that I wanted to travel during the night is so that even if I get lost, I would have a whole day to find a way out or a rescue. I arrived in Nairobi that morning and went to a public phone booth, queued and dialed the number I was given. The call did not go through. It has not gone through till now! I did not speak about it and only picked a lesson without picking a

> *He who has a why to live can bear almost any how.*
>
> *---Nietzche---*

grudge. Disappointment comes in various shapes and sizes, and more so from the people you will hardly expect to disappoint you. I know this firsthand.

Countless times, I have been disappointed by people who are very close to me. I cannot list every detail here. It could take a whole 500, 000 page book of disappointment. Surely it would not add you a lot of energy reading such a disastrous catalog of catastrophes. But perhaps I will choose to write it eventually; Disappointment 101 I would call it. Just a few are highlighted in this book to illustrate the point and to encourage you. And they are not the worst ones. I have simply selected the most appropriate ones for our case.

The weather will disappoint you.

If you doubt me, ask farmers who have experienced this, or someone who planned a wedding on a day that turned out to be a rainy day. Remember when Pope Francis visited Kenya in November 2015. The day he celebrated mass at the graduation square, University of Nairobi, it rained like never before; whole night before and all the morning. That is a classic example. People who traveled from far and wide were thoroughly drenched in a queue, waiting for the gates to be opened from as early as 3:00am. These are things beyond your control. You do not curse them, you take it easy, enjoy the disappointment and keep on.

When I was going to shoot my first official video for the talks I give, I had invited good prospects from various industries who had confirmed attendance. In my thinking, this was it! They would come and see for themselves the type of stuff we have, the type of people we are and I expected my business to take off in a big way from there henceforth. Besides, this video, which was costing me a lot of money, most of which was borrowed, was going to be sellable and, to an extent, some money would be recovered. The prospects were high. I assembled my team and we were on fire. Everything had been paid for. I would be the chief speaker. We had an entertainment segment by Joan Mugambi, a great artist and a long time friend with whom we used to sing in the University of Nairobi choir. I would have my great pal, Larry Liza, despite his ever busy schedule, to be my master of ceremony for the day. (Larry is more on air than on land; always flying to great destinations.) Expectations were very high, you see? The weather was very beautiful and promising all day long. No sign of rain could be seen; clear sky. Then what? On that particular day, that particular afternoon, it rained in Nairobi like I had never seen before! Because of my level of integrity with people, my belief was still strong that a good number would turn up. You know, sometimes, just because you hardly disappoint people, you expect them to also keep their side of the bargain. Traffic became horrible! I sank down! It never was! Just a handful turned up! Thanks to the dreadful power of the weather!

Friends will disappoint you

This is the right time to tell you this, now that we are talking about that particular event that was thwarted by the harsh storm. I have mentioned about that video which I had sacrificed so much to produce that day. The producer had been a college comrade and we were also singing in the same church choir with him during our days as university students. I had known him for long from the time he joined the university, when he graduated and got a job with a bank. He got into trouble and was sent home by the bank and then he was out of sight for long. When he re-appeared, we were still meeting in church related activities, at one point he was taking videos for our annual free medical camp organized by our church. We had shared a lot and he mentioned how he had transitioned to professional photography.

From my compassion and understanding of how tough the market can be, I tend to like promoting people I have known, because of the trust I have developed in them and more so because that would boost them in one way or the other in this rough market. So we talked and he gave me ideas and was ready and willing to do me a great work. I did not even bargain. What a mistake! At times I have that weakness. Normally I try to ensure that anyone who deals with me feels good doing business with me or working for me. So when he justified his cost, in terms of the types of lighting he would be providing, the type of cameras and all sorts of big terminologies which did not make much sense for me, I chose to entrust him with my make or break project.

> *Troubles come not to trouble you but to train you. Do not miss the lesson!*
>
> *---Otieno Paul-Peter---*

He asked for a commitment fee, down-payment, so he can secure the tools of trade in good time. I did as advised. We agreed on the date for the event and the time he had to arrive. The event was to start at 6:00pm. I am a very disciplined fellow when it comes to time. He suggested to be there before 5:00pm with his team. I started calling the guy at 4:30pm, reminding him that I am already there just to ensure things are in order. He said that he was already on his way. True! He arrived well after 6:00pm and started setting up when my few guests had arrived and we had to buy time before getting started. When we started, I kept wondering why these lights did not really resemble the picture that was painted for me; the big expensive 'flood' lights I expected. No problem! He is the expert. I have no idea. Shortly in the middle of the function, the lights went off at least twice! Leaving people in darkness!

"No big deal", he said, "I'll take good care of that when the shooting is finished."

The talk was great and all present were both pleased and inspired. The guy asked me for the balance for the shooting. I did not carry money that day. In fact, I had thought that the balance, being much less than the deposit, would be issued at the exchange of the final product. He was to give me a 45min video, an audio and some short clips for social media. He took a few still photos of me to use for the cover design of the final DVD. I had to source for money over the phone to give him because he could not leave me, that he has to pay his crew. He was going to edit and give me the final product within a week.

After about two weeks, he gave me a rough copy of 17 minutes to comment on before they finalize the product. I gave my comments; reminding him about some of the captions I had suggested prior, the duration of the video (at least 45mins), and the specific sections that he had left out but I desired to include. He promised to work on it and revert soon. I'm still waiting! My good friend promised 'real heaven' and was able to paint the marvelous picture how St. Peter is going to come with my diadem. He even did a 'mock' interview with me to add as introduction and closing comments besides taking good still-photos to help in designing the cover. Felix Muchiri, alias Ken Felix, is yet to bring me the products. Friends will disappoint you!

Employers will disappoint you:

Before I forget, let me share this one too. When I was in the university, we used to solve some mathematical problems called *Commercial Arithmetic* where students were given some figures for basic salaries, allowances, commissions, tax charts, deductions, etc and the student was asked to come up with some sort of pay slip indicating the net salary. Perhaps you remember such things. Don't you? This, in my view, was giving a glimpse into what happens in the job market, and thus what would happen if I get employed. I say 'if' because I was not really keen on being an employee. I simply could not imagine myself waiting for a whole month in order to see an income which would quickly fade away in a matter of days, leaving me with a large part of month to survive. My view, in part, was shaped by the life I saw in my dad; waiting for money hungrily and picking debts in the meantime, borrowing everything with a promise to pay when salary comes, only to disappoint other worthy creditors.

> *When we focus on our gratitude, the tide of disappointment goes out and the tide of love rushes in.*
>
> *---Kristin Armstrong---*

So when I got my first job, training ICT courses in a very prestigious institute, an organization I had really admired and desired to work with during the last part of my college life, I had expected to see and experience the stuff I had studied in *Commercial Arithmetic.* I had expected that other than the basic salary, which they said, to my amazement, was to be just USD177.00, they were going to pay me 15% house allowance, 10% transport allowance, commissions among other benefits. To start with, I expected a bigger salary, let alone the allowances. I was ignorant about how the real pay slips look like. I was glad to accept the job without asking any questions to do with the allowances because I had imagined it is the standard way. I had started working in the middle of the month, around 14th of September. Wait until I saw my pay slip. It was a big shock to me! I thought something was wrong! It could not be! A gross of USD88.00? I was surprised and became the fool of the day. I calmly and politely asked a colleague whether that was all we could expect. All these guys seemed content! Talk about disappointment! In a way, I still feel that whoever designed that *Commercial Arithmetic* owes me an apology! It is really misleading! Should you meet him/her/them, kindly pass that message appropriately.

From that company, I headed to an Internet Service Provider (ISP) Company. It was a great and prestigious organization too. The pay was much better. After about a year, one afternoon, I saw people being called one by one to the Human Resource Manager's office. Instinctively, I noticed that something was not right. It took almost 45 minutes before smelling a rat. It was about 4:00pm. A few guys had gone into the office and were coming out, looking somewhat disappointed but staying calm, heading to their work stations and picking their stuff, going home. No one was talking. No information. The following day, the news had spread. 17 colleagues had been retrenched. These were people who still had great hopes, perhaps, to build their careers in the company and take care of their families. They woke up with jobs, they went to sleep jobless. That is disappointment!

Here is a classic one I love, a friend with whom we were in graduate school was retrenched from another company and had to drop his studies. But that just began his journey to greatness! He later got another job with an international company where he worked briefly before going it alone. He went ahead and built his own firm. After a while, the business picked well and now doing great; employing tens of people. Employers will disappoint you! How you take that disappointment is what will determine your future.

The first time I read the popular book, Think and Grow Rich by Napoleon Hill, was during a hardship moment for me. My business was doing badly and not much excitement was left within me. My philosophical mind had started analyzing and digesting what could be wrong. I was quickly becoming lethargic and life was not very tasteful. I had just began looking for answers. I sincerely cannot remember how the title for this book. Neither do I know where I got it from. But the book, in soft copy, landed in my hands (or should I say my laptop?) and I started reading it. One of the statements I remember from that particular book till now and one that keeps me always going no matter what, is this:

Old man, Failure,
is always on the path to success,
waiting for those who fail the persistence test.
----Napoleon Hill----

That is the day I made a firm resolution with myself. I chose to stay on course no matter what happens and to pass the great test of persistence. The great words of Margaret Ogolla, in her book, *The River and The Source*, talking about a certain Akoko Obanda Nyar Imbo who knew not the meaning of quitting, sunk deep in my mind! I would never be a quitter! And so should you! Stay on!

You will be disappointed by Death:

Death of some of the people who could be very instrumental in your business, career or family life and success will disappoint and devastate you. People who are really critical to your Living the Dream. That is life! I have seen that *many* times. I know you have heard many such stories yourself and perhaps you have experienced some. It surprises me less nowadays because I learnt that it is the way of life. May be you loose the person responsible for your school fees, sponsorship, rent or upkeep. But never should that bother you! You will learn to say, "*even this will not stop me because I am unstoppable!*" You will need a great degree of mental toughness and emotional strength. Pick up the pieces and move on. Disease is also a major source of disappointment. Bill Gates, for instance, had to let his friend and co-founder of Microsoft, Allen Paul, to resign prematurely when he got crippled and bogged down by an incurable disease. Allen had to forfeit his stake in the then upcoming industry giant Microsoft.

The other sources of your disappointments shall include systems, machines, siblings, your results, your attitude, and level of knowledge. This is why it is important that we keep on studying every single day of our lives. We can scarcely exhaust the list and, besides, it is not really healthy for your attitude. But my sole purpose here is to infuse in you an attitude of resilience; a healthier response to such scenarios. That you may afford to stay calm and smile at the face of disappointments; knowing that they are good for you; making you wiser, stronger and more mature. Making you to qualify for the success that you want. They give you the bigger reason to pursue your aspirations and Live Your Dream!

Results hardly come fast. Nature prevents us from seeing everything at the onset. I remember listening to Brian Tracy, a renown speaker and author, talking about this. It made much sense for me because my journey was on. I was experiencing lots of turbulence in my life. During such times, you will wonder if there is still hope left. But he said,

"..somehow, nature has a way to hide from us the hurtful experiences in entire journey when we are just starting." And this is because if you could see in advance the troubles you are going to pass through, some how you may choose to quit before you get started. Why, because, by nature, man fears work, let alone criticism, disappointments, difficulties.

Now comes the grim truth; the success you are presumably looking for will hardly show up that fast! Sometimes fear creeps in, uncertainty, excitement and you keep pursuing and pursuing. I insist; success is very timid, shy and meek. You must really do the work of seduction and winning her over. On the other side, failure is very aggressive, self-driven, brave and go-getter. You do not have to invite him to come. He will come in and lodge with you even without your permission as long as an opportunity crops up. He will gate-crash! If not taken seriously, this old man called failure will give you the greatest fight. Learn and use the acquired weapons to win the war. This book equips you with all that.

Again, when your success is just around the corner, that is when you are going to meet them all. Lest you forget!

Disappoint the Disappointments

That is the best advise I can give you when it comes to disappointments; disappoint the disappointments! I know of no better way to handle the disappointments than treating them to their own medicine; disappointing them! And by discipline, you can disappoint the disappointments. In order to do this, you must make up your mind to do it in the first place. Making up your mind is the first major step and do not expect anyone to cheer you up when you are at it. That is actually what should make success so exciting and exhilarating. If everyone else would encourage you then it would not be as sweet, I want to believe. You must choose to run against the storm like an eagle. No much company at this point; at least in decision making and action.

Now that you have made up your mind to disappoint the disappointments, that does not mean you focus on them. Remember, they will certainly come and you must not resist them. That would go against the law of non-resistance. Yours is to discipline your thoughts to an extent that you will not even notice them as real disappointments but rather as some minor setbacks on the way to correct your initial poor judgments or planning. You know one thing that I learnt? If you already know that problems will come, they will not surprise you when they come. At least you will have some attitude of resilience and you will overcome them. But that is only possible if you are disciplined enough in terms of your focus, thoughts, habits, talks...that simply means you become a disciplined person.

Learn to disengage in negative thinking. Learn to shift your focus, whenever it wants to tell you how terrible things are, to a positive wavelength. Learn to take charge of your mind, lest you lose all the required energy to drive you across your Jordan. Negativity is the greatest opponent you will have to fight. The battle is in the mind. It is spiritual, not physical. You must work harder on yourself in order to disappoint your disappointments. You must keep on killing your older self and getting reborn anew every single day. You must be determined to take your daily dose of reading, motivation and learning. You must keep the right company lest you shift into the danger zone. You must keep your daily regimen of exercise. For some reason, people who are physically fit tend to be mentally fit as well. And they are hardly negative. A lazy body begets a lazy mind. Thinking right is hard work. It could be the only work. But with practice, over time, it becomes much simpler and more exciting. Keep on keeping on in your struggle to purify your mind.

I am always excited about this discovery of the mind! The more I speak about it, the more it amazes me! Very complex yet simple in operation.. Hard to understand but simple to use. But for greater results, one must persist in a disciplined fashion. Or else, the results would be unpleasant.

You will, also, need to eat the right diet. A good diet contributes massively to the development of your mind and attitudes. Health only gets complete when you think of it wholesomely. Diet is an indispensable discipline. It is good for your body and your mind. In my informed opinion, taking care of your body is your own responsibility; not your doctor's. Many people, however, pay little attention to this.

We are a generation that is used to passing the buck. And one reason we like doing this, I believe, is because we do not want to be blamed. Neither do we like to get tired.

Centuries past, the concept of nutrition was relatively foreign and less attractive. We must understand that as the world develops, new challenges emerge. I learnt a long time ago that every time you solve one problem, you create another. By solving the problem of waiting for too long for food to be ready, and creating more jobs through fast food industry and fertilizers and the likes, we have created health challenges. It is now that the concept of nutrition cannot be ignored; especially if you have a dream. You must learn how to eat right in order to think right, act right and live right. And there is no shortcut to it.

I hereby charge you to read the books about health and nutrition. Ignorance is no defense here, just as before the law. In fact, ignorance has never been an excuse as far as I'm concerned. Why? Because *"people perish due lack of knowledge."* And we have discussed this at length.

In brief, your physical health has three main elements and none is more superior to the other. You need rest, you need a good diet, and you need exercise. Again, I say, everything in moderation. As Robin Sharma says in his best selling book, The Monk Who Sold His Ferrari, it is not the quantity of sleep but the quality. So you do not have to sleep for 10 hours to be healthy. You could have ten hours of troubled sleep, which is not healthy. Better have four hours of deep sleep instead. Then you need at least 90 minutes of exercise in a whole week. Is that hard? Not at all. Just three times a week, you can take a brisk walk for 30 minutes, enough to make you pant and that would be sufficient. If you can walk up the flight of stairs, the better.

> *The size of your success is measured by the strength of your desire, the size of your dream and how you handle disappointments along the way.*
>
> *---Robert Kiyosaki---*

We had talked about this under Disciplined Diet in Chapter 3. You can refer. Notice the word 'discipline' coming in again? Yes! The medicine for disappointments. Perhaps I need to also say that it is important to observe your weight; ensuring you have the right Body Mass Index (BMI). There is nothing fancy in being either underweight or overweight. These present health challenges.

Take care of your spiritual health. Lest I forget to tell you, the battle is more spiritual than physical. Your spirit determines almost everything in your life. So learn to feed your spirit because that, actually, is whom you are. This happens when you connect to the universe through meditation and prayer, reflection and study. If you belong to a certain spiritual/religious group, with values that include love, forgiveness, faith and hope, it would help. Follow your heart, here. What seems peaceful and soothing to your mind and soul. All of us, mankind, are bestowed with universal powers that can only be properly appropriated if we unite with the Omnipotent source. I am not a preacher, at least for now, but all these contribute immensely into building your stamina to withstand the strong winds of disappointments and discouragements.

Here is another invaluable idea. Every single point of disappointment must not be allowed to go without harnessing the good with which it comes. You must know, and always remember, that every single point of disappointment has an appointment within it. There must always be something good which lurks therein. Yours is to seek it and mine it. A real winner must learn to mine this gold. It keeps you focused and positive. Only losers do not learn from a trouble-spot. All successful people do and that is why they come out even much wiser and stronger. You will have to learn to be fascinated instead of being frustrated with such low moments when things do not tend to work as planned. Find something to get excited about and look at the bigger picture. What can you learn from it? How can you benefit from that experience and make profit for your future decisions and activities? That is a worthy question to ask at this particular time. Else, you lose double! That means, you lose in the pains of disappointments themselves and lose the lesson. You really do not want to be that loser!

Another point, very closely related to the above is this, know that for everything under the sun, there are seasons. This concept of seasons is going to assist you understand that you must go through the full cycle and then allover again until the end of times.

> *We must accept finite disappointment but never lose infinite hope.*
>
> *---Martin Luther King, Jnr.---*

There are planting seasons, harrowing, weeding, harvesting, raining, drought and many other seasons. A human life has got its seasons as well; not only as a community or a group, but also individually. You can't harvest every season. This concept of seasons is also called TIMING. There is a time for everything. That should help you know that after recession comes depression and after depression comes recession and the cycle continues. That means if you are in a recession now, your depression is coming and vice versa. Don't you see that after night comes day and a night follows a day? Yea, that is the way the universe is ordered. What can you do about it? What can a man do! Not much! We accept the reality, cope with it and build our mental toughness.

All these should inform you that no problem will persist forever. You either shall, if you persist, have to achieve what you want or quit. But quitting automatically makes you a loser, and off-course, makes the problem your lifestyle. A change in strategy is acceptable. But not throwing in the towel! At least for people with dreams! So you are only left with two choices, succeeding or succeeding.

Napoleon Hill said, in his greatest book, Think and Grow Rich, that success will come to you at unexpected times and in so large a magnitude, if you persist, that you will certainly wonder where the hell it had been lurking all the while when you were looking for it in tears and pains. You will be renewed and rejuvenated. You will forget the past troubles. You will see The TOP! And definitely Live at THE TOP! Disappoint your disappointments! You can do it!

Shock Absorbers

Here is something else I learnt a long time ago; leave room for shock absorbers. Do not allow your heart to be broken. Accept certain realities and if, for example, an idea pops in your mind of a possibility of a tragedy occurring, do not preoccupy your mind with worry about how distressed you would be or how terrible things would be if it happens. Just allow two percent or so chance that it can happen and figure out how you would deal with it calmly. Do not allow yourself to be a problem focused person, but rather, a solution focused person. Putting up mitigation measures or having several options. My experience has always been that close to 50% of the time, you will need the second option because the first one will not work.

By setting up strategies to deal with the unlikely situations of disappointments, by having a plan B and even C, you are giving yourself a shock absorber, which is a term I learnt from automobile machines having some springs to lessen the impact should it hit an object or a pothole. Life works like that. It is not being negative to put a shock absorber, it is being real. People will disappoint you again and again. Truth be told, there are really nasty people living on planet earth. They may be good in language and sincerely looking harmless. But watch your back. Do not trust everyone. If you over rely on what they say and the promises they give, you may have heart attack. Have for yourself a shock-absorber.

For along time this had been my weakness. It has been a real undoing in my life. I tend to trust people at their word. For some reason, I do not expect people to lie or to just do things considered morally wrong. More so if they look descent. But this has costed me fortunes. Time and again I have been a victim of my own folly. As Donald Trump would put it, animals would kill for food, but there are human beings who will kill you for sport! In my life, I did not like the word 'enemy'. Neither did I believe in it. I believed that I cannot be someone's enemy because I also hold no grudge, which is, religiously, a good thing. But much as I know that I may not have an enemy, I have come to realize that I could be an enemy to some people for whatever reason. Notice that if you are (or if you try to be) good, you are a possible enemy to the 'evil' ones; the corrupt, the mischievous, the lazy etc for very obvious reasons. If you are evil, you are also a possible enemy to the well-mannered. That alone should be enough to make you someone's enemy. Someone who will celebrate your success with you, perhaps, as a friend, in the light, and behind you work extra hard to ensure you fail. It helps to have some shock absorbers.

> *Disenchantment, whether it is a minor disappointment or a major shock, is the signal that things are moving into transition in your life.*
>
> *---William Throsby Bridges---*

"*Judge them by their fruits*", the bible says, "*not by their words.*" Revisiting an earlier narration about my Mombasa expedition, at the start, I was still too young and naive. No one had taught me these things. Neither had life itself shared such an insight. I remember writing a telegram, which at that time was one of the fastest means of communication, that he should pick me at the railway station. He had promised to take me to (secondary) school. Not only did he fail to come pick me from the station, he also never bothered about the story of schooling me. Never! One of my earliest disappointments and glimpse to reality. But I still did try my best to understand his position and respected it. He was a good man. You can imagine being in a town as vast as Mombasa, the second largest in Kenya also situated along the coastline, when you are from an inland village and then no one picks you from the bus stop, and no phones! Thank GOD, at least for this, someone gave me a shock absorber. His own uncle, in Kisumu, where I had to pass-by in order to be escorted and assisted into the train, cautioned me against expecting to be picked, and his reasoning was noble; how about if he had not gotten the telegram. Perhaps because he had not gone to his mailbox at the post office! He pitied me and was worried for me.

"Mombasa is not a village where you can stand and call out someone's name then they hear you and respond. You cannot possibly ask for someone by name at the railway station unless the person you are looking for works there!" Those were his shocking remarks to me. In my little mind, I had only imagined a village sort-of scenario where anyone you ask can guide. Remember I was not aware about how people live, in terms of housing, in urban areas. Neither did I have an idea about the exact estate where my would-be host lived. Talk of ignorance!

In order to assist me, the old man scurried for some fixed telephone numbers to give me that I would call in case I reach and no one shows up for me. These were for some of his sons and acquaintances in this many centuries old town. To start with, I had not thought that I would need to eat on the way. The journey would take two days by train. I did not even have a coin to make such calls, let alone for food. And had I told you that up till then I had never made a phone call from a booth? I, therefore, even dreaded doing it! Lest I make a mistake and break them and get arrested!

About six years later, when I came to Nairobi for the first time, to revise the courses for my university admission, the person who promised to pick me and even gave me his mobile phone number, thank GOD there were already mobile phones, also did a similar thing; he never picked the call. He has not picked it till now. I never saw him and never even learnt where he stays. GOD knows why! I really have no idea if the phone number I was given was accurate. But he later passed on, may GOD rest his soul in peace. My plan B worked this time around, against my expectation. So, trust me if I say, expect some real challenges and it is wise to put up some shock absorbers and never to expect much from others. It will serve you well to rely on your own initiative, effort and, if you are religious, which is a great thing, your God. I am religious myself and I am very proud of it. Do not expect free rides!

Lastly, remember my story about video shooting. Where my friend, Ken disappointed me. I had trusted him so much that we did not have any written contract, against my mentors and lecturer's advise, nor did he issue me with a receipt. He did not deliver. He is yet to. Actually he is yet to talk to me. I did not organize for any backup. I had to relearn this lesson again; shock-absorbers and plan Bs.

I can tell you story after story about this and still we will not finish. But the point is home. Working without thinking of plan B will put you into jeopardy. It is never wise!

Listening Again

In this disappointment part also, listening to your heart will help a great deal. Why? Because your heart will hardly lie to you despite the facts and figures. Your heart also knows pretty well what is good for you. GOD made success not to be so easy to get in order that you may grow for you to achieve it. That you may work on it and qualify for it. That you may appreciate it when you finally achieve it. There is no much glory in doing things that everyone else can do well. But it takes following your heart in order to be great! You may, for example, follow your intellect and become a great lawyer with a lot of money but very empty in your heart. Because your heart, perhaps, who wanted you to be a teacher, never got satisfied by your intellectual choice of law. And you, perhaps, in being a teacher, you could be much happier, greater and more successful. And you could still be a teacher, teaching law. If your heart cautions you about something, listen and follow. Something told me to ask for a receipt from my friend, but I felt it would simply mean I do not trust him which would not reflect well on our relationship. I ended up getting hurt. Follow your heart. Trust your heart and your conscience. You will be happy indeed, and Live Your Dream!

The Law of Forgiveness

Here is something that I consider very essential to know. And I am not a preacher, neither do I want to become one. I am just a teacher of life lessons, passionate about sharing what I have learnt to work and what works not. Forgive! You may ask yourself how failing to forgive will stop you from Living Your Dream! My answer is, in many possible ways! It has stopped others and could still do to you.

> *The weak can never forgive. Forgiveness is an attribute of the strong.*
>
> ---*Mahatma Gandhi*---

Forgiving, in my very considered opinion, may look really stupid and weak. Anyone who chooses to forgive normally looks like a weakling or a loser. But there is a lot of greatness in that lowliness. And I do not mean surrender. I do not mean that you let go because you have no choice. I mean you choose to forgive despite having multiple options through which to get even. Whenever you do not forgive, because people are going to annoy you anyway, and take you for a ride in many ways, you hurt your feelings. Simply learn to let go and feel great in doing so. If you do not, you are the one getting more hurt and delaying your own achievements. This concept is so deep that in many cases few people want to explain it. But in my 'theory of everything', this is going back to the element of thought, activity and results. Where we said your thoughts are composed of your knowledge and feelings; what you know and what you feel. Your feeling is very essential for your achievement. You cannot feel bad and get good results just like you cannot plant maize and harvest beans. It is not possible. It is the law of sowing and reaping.

When your heart is heavy with the burden of hate, there is no room for peace and creative thinking. Creative thinking that begets good results. Letting go allows you to let go of the feelings as well, thereby allowing you to take care of the most important asset you have; your mind! Once this is done in the best possible way, you will be at a receptive frequency for the blessings from above. Whatever that means to you. I hope I made myself clear. This, therefore, means that by holding grudge, you are hurting yourself even more than the person you are holding the grudge against, while you are already hurt by the guy anyway. You are even losing your own time, energy and health. Worry and bad feelings spend more mental energy from you that could be used in more productive engagements. It could, as well compromise your physical health.

> *Always forgive your enemies. Nothing annoys them so much.*
>
> *---Oscar Wilde---*

Lest I be taken out of context, get to know that forgiving does not necessarily amount to obstructing the course of justice. That does not mean that if someone is a murderer, so forgiving him means releasing him from prison. It only means that you stop feeling bad about what they did to you. This is not an easy task. To Christians, it would mean spiritual forgiveness where you do not dwell on the past anymore, and start praying for them and wishing them well. Generally, this can be achieved by giving the offender the benefit of doubt, sometimes tying to think how you could have handled the same scenario if you were in his/her shoes.

Forgiving brings a lot of good to you. There is a legend story to teach about this act; *"whatever you do to them...you do it to me"*. I could go on and on to explain some deep sense in this, but I feel it would steal our focus. Just remember one simple thing that this book is focusing more on trying to train your emotions and help you develop a kind of emotional intelligence, mental toughness and highest level of resilience that enable you to Live Your Dream. That is why I am trying to seal any leakage of positive energy from you and blocking any window of negative energy towards you.

Your Source of Fuel

The only fuel that will keep you positive and steer you away from the distractions is your goal. Your ultimate chief aim. That particular dream that you want to achieve. That is your motivation and it must, therefore, be inspiring enough that you can actually taste it in your mind before it really comes physically. Feed your mind with the imagination of what it is going to be like when you achieve it and feel the feeling. Let your body and soul sock itself in that feeling as oftentimes as possible since that is the only way you will keep your focus and get the energy required in the battlefield of Living Your Dream! If you have enough 'why', then the 'how' will show up and the stamina to push for it will be there. Enjoy the journey and the disappointments. Again, in the wording of Jim Rohn, "make frustrations become fascinations". Find a reason to appreciate every setback. At every point of setback, scheme again, adjusting your plans appropriately then move on wiser and stronger.

> *What keeps me going is goals.*
>
> *---Mohamed Ali---*

Need For Genuine Help

This is a very important point. It is never a weakness as many would want to think. Asking for help is a sign of strength. Now, I have no idea whether you believe in GOD or not. But I do. And part of my belief is that, GOD has a major role to play in the path of your success. GOD does the works that are within His domain to do. You do what is within your power to do. Everyone has to do his/her part in cultivating success and leave the rest for GOD. He does not work alone. And He does not do your work either. He surely works through you and others to assist you. But whether you want to call that luck, universe or whatever, I refer to Him as GOD; that universal power who seems to be the cause and source of all things. Without Him we would not be talking about the laws of nature. Otherwise, who established them?

At one time when I was doing my last year of secondary education, when I went back to school after such a long time outside, having lost all the previous notes and class work, I was starting afresh. Time was not on my side and every encouragement was necessary. One of my teachers, who used to teach history, said; "you must do your part so that GOD can do His part. You must do the work, read and revise, which is your part of the bargain. Only then will GOD assist you to pass."

> *Do not be anxious about anything, but in everything by prayer and supplication with thanksgiving make your requests known to God.*
>
> *---Philippians 4:6---*

This made a lot of sense for me and I could not help imagining how GOD would make me know something I had not read in a book and revised. That is the time I learnt about this sort of magnificent cooperation with the Almighty. If I read and revise, He will enable me to remember. Again, He may make the exams that come fall squarely on the areas I have mastered, I thought to myself. He may give me the spirit of courage, instead of fear, and even keep me in good enough health to be able to take the exams. Bad things happen, and that is why when we pray the Lord's prayer, 'Our Father…', we say along the way '..but deliver us from all evil'. At least, that we may stay safe and sound. It is also critical in mastering your emotions.

> *Time spent in prayer is never wasted.*
>
> *---Francis Fenelon---*

It is therefore prudent that you do what you can do and let GOD do what only He can do. If you plant, GOD enables the rain to come and causes the plant to grow; not to rot in the soil. He may also protect you from any injury as you go about working in your garden so that you are able to accomplish your work in good time for the rains and keep you long enough to reap the benefits. This analogy works for every area of trade. You could be a trader, you still need the protection from the burglars and thugs. You need some divine providence that your merchandise may sell, perhaps much quicker. Some things will happen that you can only explain if you include GOD in the equation. So, without expounding much on this, just know that GOD has a major role to play in your success and happiness. And once that has happened, remember to thank Him.

This thanksgiving bit, is equally very essential and therapeutic. It helps you to develop that good feeling which is very essential for you to achieve the good results. I hope you will understand these interconnections. It helps to be thankful in every situation, and to always speak and think good. By thanksgiving, you get to feel great.

Chapter 5

DETOUR

GIVE principle

As I continue my study on the philosophy of human potential, I have come to appreciate that you cannot expect the journey to be straight or smooth. It will be full of detours. Lots of enticing things and of lesser value will present themselves in various manner. This may include a promotion in your current position, a trip abroad or a new opportunity beckoning elsewhere. The list is long. They will seduce you and steal your appetite for pursuing and Living Your real Dream! Detours can also present themselves in terms of persecutions and afflictions, lack of support from key stakeholders, divorce, and anything that would make you choose to surrender. In that regard, I have also included, in this short book, this chapter of Detour so that I may take sometime to discuss with you some of the few lessons to grant you 'food for the journey'; keeping you well nourished on your path to big accomplishments.

After careful analysis and study using my data mining and knowledge discovery principles, I came up with a fundamental strategy that can help summarize the principles discussed so far. Allow me to take you back a little. This is a ready-to-use tool that you can, always, keep with you everywhere no matter what your goal may be.

At one point in time, having evaluated life on my own , then, more limited thinking, I acquired a belief that life tends to give one what he/she wants. In fact I had to put it this way, even without sharing with people then for lack of confidence, that life is like a polygon; a many-sided figure, with each side of the figure representing a particular lifestyle. One simply needs to tilt this polygon, choosing which side to face him/her and whichever the lifestyle that particular side represents, that becomes his/hers. For some reason I had that belief that man is not helpless. Nothing like some preordained path without our participation and active cooperation. I know this is contestable in some quarters. But with such few exceptions like in any other rule, man has all the free-will. This was just born out of my own contemplation. But I could not prove it, nor share it with people. Who was I? A little village boy without a sign of success and seemingly no chance of even a middle-class, to share such an insight! To an extent I desired to prove it by Living my Dream. So, along the way, it came to pass that I found some proof to 'my philosophy'.

Something amused me during my second year of study at the university. The belief was already firm in my heart, though. Normally I can take quite long, years for that matter, with a thought in my heart upon which I ponder and meditate, striving for a satisfying answer. And that is how this came to be. So, during my second year I once entered a particular hall of residence, we called them hostels. I was pressed and went to the washroom in that particular hall to relieve myself. Hall six, it was, I still remember. And at the urinal where I stood doing my business, I looked straight and saw some writing on the wall in pink color, it said, "*at this very moment, your future is in your hands*". I could not resist laughing at this grim joke! I felt somewhat excited about the idea that my future is in my hands. It communicated to me something I wanted to hear despite what the writer implied,...that's what amused me! Do not laugh alone if you got the joke. But besides the joke, take it from me, it is not just at certain moments but rather always. Your future is always in your hands, at least to a large extent. You can do anything you want with it. This is an absolute statement of truth.

How, then, besides all that we have said so far, can you shape your future? We have talked of your thoughts. We have talked of your feelings, your knowledge, activities, much more. What then could be left! Nothing much peculiar. The only thing I want to add here is a formula that can bring everything else in perspective and give you a clearer steering wheel. It is, if you wish, a short version of what you have covered so far, but very important. This is the reason so many people, even after reading so many books, find it difficult to implement. For that reason, here is a way you can start implementing some of the principles from now on more deliberately. I sure hope that you have grasped much from the discussions so far and are well on your way to Living Your Dream, that you have started working on ideas you learnt in previous chapters. So here is just another help you may consider as a reinforcement.

I now GIVE you this key to control your destiny. Kindly remember the word GIVE all your life. Remember it everywhere every time because upon it lies everything you want to know. GIVE is the word of CONTROL! You will use it the rest of your life. Every successful person uses it in some form, knowingly or otherwise. Unsuccessful people also do, only poorly and in ignorance! Just like a baby can use a razor. You too, most certainly, have been using it only that you, perhaps, so far, did it in ignorance and got the painful side of it. This is not a FAITH question. It is the result of years of study and analysis of life and lives, books and people, thoughts and philosophies. I being the most important specimen. So what does this simple word, GIVE, really mean? How will you use it?

'**G**', which is the first letter of that word, is for GOALS. Never live a goalless life! Always know where you are headed or, at least, where you want to go. It will help you a lot. Have a clear idea about what you want in life, if not yet, from now on. Take some few days and get pretty clear about your life, the career path you intend to follow, the type of person you want to become, the type of family you want to have, the more the details, the better for you. This is a way to optimize, to your advantage, your most important tool, your mind! Without this information, you will get whatever else is occupying your mind! Why? Because your mind cannot be blank! Nature abhors a vacuum and so it will certainly feed something else and most of the times it is fear, worry, anxiety and all that you do not want. That is the weed in the world of mind. Now I have told you! Know what you want and make it clear. Doing this is going to make the biggest difference in your life. Ensure you are clear about everything including, where applicable, the taxi/matatu you are going to use next. If a garden is left unattended, will it remain blank? Not really! Will something useful come out of it? Not quite often! The useless weeds are the once that welcome themselves and start lodging in. Protect your mind by filling it up with what is useful to you.

> *Goals are the foundation for success.*
>
> *---Otieno Paul-Peter---*

I really do not mean to say it is easy! No! It will take time and practice. But if that is all you will be able to do, you will certainly have a better chance of Living Your Dream! The battle will have been won close to 70%. Trust me! Just commit to catching yourself thinking wrong things and changing your thoughts instantly. The simplest way for me to achieve this is just being deliberate and conscious about my thoughts.

'**I**' is for Inspire or Inspiration. Here is the other very critical point. It is the ignition key. That is, let everything you are putting down as your goal be inspiring to you. Something that can 'make you run'! It turns your inside into excitement. This is very important more so when it comes to setting life goals, life purposes, the type of dreams you have in your mind. Without this bit, you probably will change them many times along the way and that would interfere with the effectiveness of this system. Besides, you will not be able to pass the test of the 2nd D, which is Determination.

> *Everything you can imagine is real.*
>
> *---Pablo Picasso---*

'**V**' is for visualization. You will have to be able to visualize yourself as having already achieved that which you want. That which is your goal. If you cannot visualize this, it may be difficult to generate the necessary feelings. And that means, therefore, that it shall, definitely, be difficult to achieve what you want. In other words, your level of desire is not yet sufficient to compel the universal forces to obey your Will. But you may attain this through P&C; practice and concentration! Practice and practice and practice this art of concentration until you are able to achieve that level of concentration and can manipulate your feelings through these visual effects. Again, some pictorial representation of the same on your wall or your pocket book or laptop may help you generate this, or some photos in your album. It is pure imagination. The mind thinks in pictures, remember! Not numbers, not words.

'**E**' stands for Emotion. Everything that is going to come to pass must, in some way, get into your emotions. Take the 'motion' part and see it as the actual movement from where you are to your goal. That means without it you will stay exactly where you are no matter what! That is not very easy; staying where you are. That is like the second Newtonian Law of motion; an object will stay at rest or keep moving in the same manner unless compelled to act otherwise by an external force. It is a great thing if your mind can stand still. But we all know it is not easy to achieve that. In fact, we call it self-mastery if you have become absolutely in charge of your mind.

> *If you can see it, you can seize it!*
>
> *---Unknown---*

Things that do not exist, once are already clear in the mind, are brought to existence through the power of emotions. Prayers work in this exact way. Just saying a prayer is not enough if you cannot emotionalize it. So, as you visualize the goal, feel it as well and you will be sure to achieve it. Even accidents work like that! It is said that nothing works without premeditation. No spontaneity. You are free to contest this. But be sure to try the concept before you contest it. Not everyone does believe this the first time, but over time, they do.

GIVE it is! Take control and start seeing miracles happening; exciting results! This will work in all realms of life whether it is health, growth, business, relationship, name it! Just try and see. It is a lifelong endeavor and our levels of achievement purely depend on our ability to appropriately use this key in our progress toward our goals.

Whatever you have learnt in the previous chapters, added to this very chapter, you are supposed to have taken care of your destiny. I will add one more thing, though.

No One Does It Alone

You are going to require a bit of help along the way! Never be too ashamed or too proud to ask for help. It works! Put it in your mind that most of the troubles you are going to face are not new at all. Others have faced them (including myself) and written about them or, at least, are willing to help if asked. Do not let pride sabotage your progress. Notice that EGO causes downfall. It has been said that 'pride comes before a fall'. GOD Himself hates the proud. So stay humble, authentic and open minded. Do not assume that you know it all. You will never ever know it all in the school of success. Learning is continuous. No one has known it all. Everyone keeps learning, everyone is a student and a student is also a teacher; teaching those on the journey with him and sharing experiences with the older and the younger. Why? Because experiences are usually very unique! One thing I learnt, unlike what is commonly imagined, successful people are willing to share information and the knowledge that has helped them to become whom they are. You will find this to be true. They are not jealous. They are not envious. As I once discovered, it is good to take successful people for dinner. Jim Rohn put it nicely in his classic audio called Personal Growth. He said, "..poor people ought to take rich people for dinner. .. but guess what, poor people keep thinking that the rich are already rich and thus should be the ones to buy dinner. This is wrong." Jim was right.

It is also good to know that the more people become successful, the more open they are to listening and learning. They hardly despise ideas or people. They give audience irrespective of who is speaking. One who is really successful is not overcome by pride, but full of respect and humility. Those who display arrogance are not really confident about themselves and are not as successful as they would want you to believe. The arrogance is sugarcoating and showoff. For this reason, if I see a person driving a more luxurious vehicle than mine, I give them respect and I expect them to be more respectful and responsible. If I see someone with more money than me, I know he/she has grown more than me in leadership and expect them to be full of decorum that comes with their stature. That is the way life is. If you meet the arrogant type, they are the wrong people who, in most cases, got the wealth they seem to have inappropriately, or inherited it, and usually will not stay at the top. The reason is simple. They have not learnt how to climb to the top. They do not know how to stay at the top either. They have bypassed the discipline.

Let me be clear here, success is not necessarily in terms of monetary wealth, but in many other areas too. Someone can be successful even if he is not blessed with material possessions. If he is happy with his life and is living his life's purpose, he is by all means very successful. Dreams are different. At all economic levels one can Live his Dreams. Do not belittle anyone's dream. What may be important to me may not be to you. What may be a lot to me may be little to another. One time I made a statement I still believe in; the level of our achievements shall only be limited by the size of our dreams. It is true.

There are people I call successful failures. These are people who acknowledge where, why and how they failed and are willing to share their experiences. Old people are very good at this, looking back into their lives and sharing their bad decisions as a warning. Do not despise them. Listen and learn from them too. Ask them questions. And make your own conclusions.

When I was preparing for my final examinations in secondary school, working to attain university grades, I asked my friends who were preparing for the same exams for the second attempt, having failed in their first attempt, and they told me what, in their opinion, caused them to fail and together we were able to work and pass very well because of the insight gained from their 'bad' experience. I really do believe that wise people can learn from anyone, anywhere. One reason is that they are blessed with an excellent attitude. And whenever I give talks about listening, I mention this too. That even when a mentally challenged person is talking and you listen keenly, some of his words will make sense for you, not necessarily for him, and you may pick some fundamental life truth from that heap of rubbish that comes from his mouth. Now that is very important for you; the listening skill. Practice listening or you will not be able to learn. And do not have a preconceived opinion or a certain answer that you expect. Have an open-mind and listen keenly then evaluate. Let whatever you pick be the subject of your own conclusion. No one can bulldoze you into doing exactly what they say, including me in this book. Chew the ideas and act on them

> *Wealth gained dishonestly dwindles away, but the one who gathers little by little will become rich.*
>
> *---Proverbs 13:11---*

as you may deem fit.

Therefore, if you find a successful person, more so someone living the kind of life you want, doing the kind of things you would want to do, then make friends with him/her and ask questions. Ask for help. Les Brown says, *"ask for help not because you are weak, but because you want to remain strong. Ask for help and do not stop until you find it!"* I love that! Whether his own or he borrowed it from elsewhere is immaterial. And your help can come from very unfamiliar sources. So do not look down on anyone. Speaking out and sharing will help. Some of the best solutions of life have come from very unexpected sources. I am reminded of an engineering idea that came from a cleaner when she was being pushed to give room for the engineers to dig the floor to extend the elevators and she asked them, concerned only about her clean piece of work and possible horrible debris, why they could not do it outside and that became the advent of making lifts protruding outside. You see?

> *The best advice I can give to anyone who is going through a rough patch is to never be afraid to ask for help.*
>
> *---Demi Lovato---*

Look for someone or people who can help you along the way as a mentor (or mentors). It will make the journey more manageable. Two are better than one. A cord made of three strands is definitely stronger. And much of the help you are looking for can also be found in books, seminars, videos and other sources. Indeed if you seek, you will find.

Where To Start

Do not wait for the best time to start. By now, you are already late. You ought to have started when you were born. As , I'm told, Winston Churchill once said, "*time is always ripe to do what is right*". Start now the way you are where you are. You are never too young to start. Neither are you too old to get started, too stupid, too clever, too short, too tall. Nothing. Do not wait till the next morning, next season, next salary advance, next Olympic games, whatever. Whatever you can do today, do it today. I have this policy; let tomorrow come to find you doing the work you are supposed to do. But do not postpone anything you can do now for another time or another day. Go right ahead with the right attitude and get going. Time keeps moving and you do not know about tomorrow. Once you lose today, it is gone! This is a painful truth! Right now as you are reading this chapter, you are already much older than when you started! If you want to know how quickly time expires, look at a stopwatch displaying how microseconds run. That is how fast you are growing older, if not wiser. But would it help if you are a wise but inactive person?

Instead of time management talks, I talk about personal management. That is because no one has a say about time! It simply moves whether you like it or not, whether you are sleeping, walking, waiting, dead or alive. Time waits no one whether president, preacher, rich, poor, clever, wise or stupid. It does not matter. Learn to cope with the time and manage yourself well, making better use of the time allocated to you, just like everyone else is allocated; 24 hours a day! No one can borrow your time that went unspent, and neither can you.

Here is another thing I find worthwhile; be tough, be aggressive. Life does not support the weak. All weak things die prematurely! Check around and become a good student of nature. Weak sperm die without fertilizing the egg, weak seedlings are removed to give room for strong ones to grow, weak athletes are gotten rid off. That is life! They call it the selection process. If you ever heard of the Concentration Camps, you must have learnt this principle. So you better be strong, be tough both physically and mentally. But more so mentally. And start now if you had not! Do not expect anything for free! Life is tough and that is why someone said, "*survival for the fittest.*" Which to me means the fit and the fitter do not survive! It is only the fittest! You better be one of the fittest, and you can be!

Chapter 6

DETOX

Be Ware: The Natural Break-pads

The lesson will be incomplete if I do not include this chapter. In pursuing your dream, there are three natural toxins that will act like your break-pads whenever you want to take a positive step. They are known to cause people to fail because of the powerful arsenal that they employ. They will make use of three really effective weapons to erect massive roadblocks to bar you from living your dreams. Would you be able to guess who the trio are? Possibly not. But I am here to let you know about them and thus fortify you enough so that you can defeat them and overcome possible hurdles they may create on your journey to success.

In the history of success, there is no other powerful

force as this; that has killed so many dreams. The members of this team work harmoniously and meticulously in executing their mission and thus form the foundation of almost all failure. They delight in your downfall and remain laughing while you are sinking. These are the greatest enemies you must defeat because there are only two choices. You either defeat them or they defeat you and defeating you means failure. Failure, in this case, means failing in life and surrendering the pursuit of your dream; making it a mirage at best. A fairy tale. It means failing to finish what you started; the race to your dreams.

> *There is only one thing that makes a dream impossible to achieve; fear of failure.*
>
> *---Paulo Coelho---*

The trio I am talking about, thus far, are Fear, Doubt and Worry. The chairman is Fear. They walk together, work together and wine together. If you notice one of them, thereabout know that the other two are, waiting to pop up or just hiding behind the curtain. I said to you that to be forewarned is to be forearmed. My intention is not only to warn you but also to arm you and ensure you do not fall into their traps.

Fear kept me from progress for long. I then started doubting my own possibility of success and doubted my opportunities, my products, my prospects and everyone who tried to encourage me. I doubted everything! I worried myself about the possibility of failure in my new business and how people would laugh and scorn at me. It hurts to feel that you are headed for failure.

Just to illustrate this point, you probably have heard of the infamous tight-rope walker who got all the excitement in doing the trick and could not wait for any such opportunity until one day a thought crossed his mind of what would happen should one day the rope breaks while he is atop. He got to worry about the next event, went ahead to keenly inspect the ropes, the type of material and the manner of tying it. All which he never bothered about before! Fear gripped him all the while dwelling on the useless thought that it is possible to fall down from the rope and die. He started to doubt himself, doubt his abilities to walk on the rope, doubted the credibility of his assistants and everything else. He dropped and died the very next time he tried it!

As I often say, Fear is very courageous and powerful. Unlike courage which is fearful and timid and thus must be nurtured and massaged, Fear requires nothing of the sort. It will rise up on its own and go after the target. That is the way it is. It was named Fear by mistake! Or so do I feel. Its attributes do not exhibit its name. You are the one to encourage your courage and frighten your Fear! Learn this and you are on the way to conquering it.

After leaving college for about a year, together with some of my friends, we had brilliant business ideas. One of the ideas was to build a cleaning company and start small.

Each one of us contributed a little cash, we registered a business, opened a bank account and the future looked great. Did we get any customer? No! Did we look for a customer? No! Why? None of us seemed ready to go look for customers who could buy our services except one, at least theoretically, because he did not do it anyway. We were too cool for such stuff like going to look for customers and, off-course, would be equally too cool to accept the benefits, I suppose. The idea died a still death! It was the same old FEAR. This time round called Fear of Rejection. Where would we be today? Only GOD knows! But you can guess, over ten years have gone by!

> *Fear is False Evidence Appearing Real*
>
> *---Unknown---*

Next, a couple of years later, I joined Network Marketing as I said before. It was a great idea whose time had come. I had tried to figure out a business I could do while still working on my full-time job until the business matures. This proved to be the best. This is because when I was leaving college, my goal was to be in business. I could not imagine myself waiting for 30 days before seeing income. I was used to income incoming all the time because in college, I ran a printing and computer services business in my hostel room. It was a nice business that kept me living a good life in college. Moving it out of college definitely required a huge amount of capital, which I had not set aside due to my myopia. And because I did not want to go live with anybody; relative or otherwise, I had to look for something to do to earn a living. Business was my first choice but having failed in ideas and capital, a job, at least a temporary job, was the quickest option. Yet, going to employment, I was determined to only go there to look for money for starting my own venture.

It did not take time before realizing that I would never get the money I required that easily. Story for another day. But you can guess! I even registered an ICT business which never picked because my job required me all the time, besides being unsure about how I would acquire customers. Again fear was a major factor in stunting this business agenda. I went back to college for a masters degree as if to kill time still trying to figure out how to be in the business world. Going back to college was good, though it is also the easiest choice which everyone seems comfortable with. It exposed me to the concept of Information Age and the Information Industries and the likes. It was at that point that Network Marketing was presented to me and I quickly realized that its attributes conformed to the information working ideology. I jumped in. I was in business as I had

> *I learned that courage was not the absence of fear, but triumph over it. The brave man is not he who does not feel afraid, but he who concurs that fear.*
>
> *---Nelson Mandela---*

wanted, and still keeping my job.

The business, I soon realized, was not going to work itself out. I had to still do my bit of selling. That is Direct Selling; a concept I belittled and hated. Till then, I had never appreciated the role of selling in entrepreneurship and success. But this would be my epiphany. It was at this point in my life that I had to FACE my FEARS and Conquer them. It took me time and effort. I studied materials and researched. I attended trainings and talks. I scurried books and meditated. I was determined to succeed and Live My Dreams. Nothing was going to stop me. I consulted my dreams and realized my desire for success was much stronger than the fear in me. I faced it and got over it! Thank GOD I did. I would not be writing this book today.

I therefore learnt the following about fear and its company:

How To Deal With Fear

1: Fear is not real!

Much as we have made it look like it is really a physical fore, it is not! Good news, right? It is imaginary and nothing else. It is like a shadow, which is appearing to be real but cannot do anything of its own. It is not invincible! Now you know. Let me explain a little.

In my meditations, I recalled when I was young and would fear walking out at night. Then later judging for myself that when I grow up I will not fear, then later starting to reason that nothing changes between day and night except that there is no sunlight and thus nothing to fear. I also started reasoning that whatever or whoever is approaching from a distance in the dark, does not really know whether I am a kid, an adult or another dangerous beast. Many such thoughts visited my mind and strengthened me. The moment I began to reason like that, the objects that would appear to be moving with me on the way at night, trailing me, and the footsteps that would follow me all ceased. Even the things that used to dance on our wall every time I was sleeping alone in our small grass-thatched hut stopped the unholy habit. The knocks I would hear on the door, the scratches at the window and the ugly dreams all went! How marvelous! This boosted me. Armed with these new thoughts, the new me started slowly talking to people about my products and it was really not as bad as my mind had made it up. No one beat me. No one insulted me. Much as very few people bought from me, many would give different excuses like, 'I don't have money at the moment', 'it is too costly', 'I don't need it now',..and the likes. And I kept moving on. A few friends would make fun of me, but I learnt to enjoy that too. It actually became exciting!

Next, I remember having a distributor in a town I had never lived in and never liked because of the horrible stories I used to hear. This big town is called Kisumu; the third largest in Kenya, East Africa. The gory stories I heard in my childhood about this town were still fresh in my mind;

ranging from insecurity to high cost of living. I was supposed to go and assist this distributor of mine to get the system right. I dreaded the mere thought of going there and kept wondering where I would sleep, where I would bathe, what I would eat there, how safe I would be in the town as I conduct my business; an elaborate litany of nonsensical scares, you see? Then another thought came to me. I remembered watching Les Brown's video and the statement he said that “Leave, and grow your wings on the way down”. I chose to leave and grow my wings on the way down. I can tell you, nothing was bad at all! I got nice places to stay in, good hotels with very descent and affordable meals,..I tell you, my friend, fear does not exist! It is not a reality. Once you go ahead to start doing that which you fear, you realize that what you fear does not exist in reality. It is fictitious. Just like watching a horror movie and fearing being alone in your own house; starting to ransack the house to be sure there is no monster. You fear for nothing! I hope you got that clear! Do not have fear.

2:Minding your business

Again I learnt that every time you are letting fear to stop you from doing what you must do, you are not minding your business. Instead, you are minding other people's businesses.

When I had just started my Network Marketing business, I was quite naive about the whole process or what it really required. As I have said earlier, the idea of selling was not pleasant to me at all. I had wanted to be a businessman but my thinking was clogged, I would say, with ego. I had been in business, but an easier type like printing in my college room which only required a few posters in the corridors of the hostels, which I would do, mostly at night, and then friends would also refer others and once I did a good job for them, more jobs came.

I had also been in the hawking business and that meant I carry merchandise and put them in a displayed manner, appetizing and so all I had to do was to hang around where prospects are and once someone saw, they would call or ask a question or two. Nothing like ice-breaking, prospecting, appointments and the likes. I guess the ice was broken already. No wonder the output was also little!

In this new business, I did not need to carry the products around and show. It was, in all honesty, unimaginable for me. I had to follow all the necessary selling processes from prospecting through closing and follow-up all the way. Can you imagine that! Good! This particular bit of the business they did not tell me when they shared with me the business plan. Perhaps I would not have gotten involved. I thank GOD they restrained! Because that would mean a different scenario for me. I would not be what I am today. So remember? Nothing for nothing! That is to say that indeed things do not just happen, they happen just.

Many times I sat down and weighed between my dreams and my fears. I had to make a choice what to go for. My desire for success was definitely stronger than my fear of failure. I made a decision to go after what I feared. It was at that point that an idea came to my mind; whose business am I doing? Whose business am I minding? Mine or someone else's? Because my fear was largely that of criticism and rejection, if I had to move on, I had to stop thinking about what others felt of me and henceforth concern myself with what I felt was good for me. In fact I remembered how I started my business for hawking sweets and the courage I mastered, remembering that it was equally hard to imagine until I got up to do it because I had to. I had to start minding my business, therefore, if I was to succeed. I did it. It helped! Mind your business!

That very moment, I remember it was in the evening, past 5:00pm and I was in the shift that would go up to 7:00pm, being relieved by the night shift. I chose to take ACTION immediately. The first target was my Human Resource Manager who was still in the office. Since he had a car, I figured out that I could sell to him a detergent for washing his car. Besides, the detergent was relatively affordable; less than $10. It was in December and many companies had actually closed for holidays. Our company was not going to close but most of my colleagues were out on long leave for Christmas and new year.

Empowered by my new belief, I gathered courage, went and smiled with the gentleman and tried to explain about the product. Tim, as we called him, did not want to buy but I insisted. He said he actually did not have the money at the moment and so I accepted to pick the money later which actually meant that he would pay when he resumes work in the new year. But I sold and learnt it is really not such a bad experience, not as bad as I had imagined. It is usually uglier in mind that in reality. That was a step in the right direction. Many others followed and my business picked. Two things, therefore, to remember: FEAR is not real, mind your business.

3:Do not expect praises..

No one is going to sing for you and cheer you up except your dreams. What is the source of your motivation. I can almost assure you that very few people will ever encourage you. You must therefore find your own dynamo. Find your own way to motivate yourself. If you fail to do this, you may quit. Reading this book is certainly one way because it is a source of encouragement. Reading books like this is a good way. Listening to the right people speaking and having a mentor will certainly help. Do not entertain negative talks from anyone. But the ultimate way to get motivated is to look at your dream! That is the reason we always insist that when you are setting a goal or when you identify your purpose or your dream, it better be something that will keep you excited and fired up every time you think of it. It will boil down to two things; you are either going for your dream or listening to nay sayers. Going for your dream or obeying your fears.

General rule, as someone once put it, "*you cannot depend on someone else to motivate you or to encourage you. What if he doesn't show up*?" That is too risky; betting all your future on someone else. Motivate yourself and find your own reasons for doing this. Your REASONS for wanting to achieve this should be your Motivation source. If you lack strong enough reasons, you will achieve nothing. As it has been said, success is 90% why and 10% how. Often times I tried to be a motivator of people in my business and realized firsthand that without self-motivation, my own motivation would not be sufficient to keep them going. It is true! I had to learn to bring out their own motivation to the surface.

If your dream is to be wealthy, how wealthy? And why? Get very clear about that. Like my reason for going out to sell was to be able to succeed in my business so I can in the long run be financially free. And my reason for financial freedom is to be able to provide for my family more than I was provided by my parents, and to assist the bright pupils who quit schooling and quit on their dreams because of lack of school fees like Nyayo and Ogaga, my primary school classmates who despite being some of the brightest in the district, could not move on; leaving their dreams shattered! And more so to prove that it is possible to achieve great success irrespective of one's background. To be an inspiration to many people who share my background. And today I am not only a great salesperson, I have taught and still teach many people to be great salespeople and how to climb the ladder of success. The power of Will! Notice that without strong enough reasons, you are also likely to be clogged with procrastination, excuses and victim mentality. Find your own motivation!

Greed, Envy & Ego

In your second phase of detox, another trio you want to eliminate are Greed, Envy and Ego. This is so critical for you that we cannot ignore it if we are really serious about you Living Your Dream! I'd like you to live your dream fully and happily, feeling fulfilled and significant. Remember my mission is to touch over a million lives positively. That is why I am so serious about giving you full info. These three are ills that if you choose to put up with, will cost you your dream and happiness. You will be disappointed and unhappy. In other words, your story will not end well. These are facts I have come to learn along the way.

Greed causes people to be unfaithful in business and life. Remember, this is not ambition. It is greed. Ambition will, mostly, lead to positive effort and thus positive results. But greed makes you more-or-less mindless, crafty and crooked. I have seen this many times. I have seen people skin their own customers because they want to reap everything from them without considering the value they are giving. Without thinking of tomorrow. It is sad! It is stupid. But it is true.

You ever heard of people who cheat in business? Take for example one who instead of selling milk, he mixes other things that look like milk, in total disregard of the safety of the substance, then sells it to unsuspecting customers with a smile, then goes home happy having made some extra money. You could take it from me, it is not how much money you made that will make you happy. It is what you did to make that money and how that money is, eventually, used for the benefit of others. Again you will never be forgiven by nature if you cheat. Nature is very unforgiving. I can forgive you. Your friends and relatives can forgive you. Even strangers can. But not nature; which is what we call life. Life is not a forgiver. Every evil you do shall find a way to come after you and painfully retaliate; causing you to pay up your dues to the last penny.

What do you think causes corruption? It is greed. No rocket science shall be required to explain that. It breaks families. It kills businesses and even causes others to kill. Same old greed. It is evil! Highly eroded level of morality. And that is what people pass on to their children. Values. It is said that it matters less what you leave for your children, but rather what you leave in them. Leave good values and ethics.

When I was in year one in the university, we used to have bible study(BS) sessions for small groups on Sunday evenings. I happened to be part of one of the groups and we went for a BS meeting at a member's room in a particular hall of residence. By nature I like keeping time. The BS meetings were meant to be starting at 7:00pm but members were often late and sometimes it would even start at 8:00pm. Every time I attend a meeting that starts late I feel pissed off, wasted and irritated. But something had caused me to stop rebelling when it comes to church affairs. I cannot explain this mystery. Perhaps just teaching me to be a sober and calm person.

> *Just like weeding frees crops from weeds and allow them to grow, so does detox get rid of weeds from you and allow you to move steadily towards your dream.*
>
> *---Otieno Paul-Peter---*

This particular evening, as usual, I was one of the first members to arrive. Shortly, another lady came in with excitement. She had finished school but was 'pirating' with a friend who was still on. The word 'pirating' was commonly used in our college by comrades/students to mean 'putting up with'. That means she would always be part of our BS group. So when she came in, she rushed to this friend of hers and exploded,

"Eh, Sophie (not real name), I came across a very exciting Insurance policy."

"Oh! How is it? How does it work?", Sophie inquired curiously.

"When you take it, the moment you start paying your

monthly premiums, it is valid irrespective of the maturity date. And should something happen that you die even the following day, they pay the beneficiaries the full amount!", she exclaimed with all her big smile.

"If you get your husband to take that, you kill him immediately after and get that money!" is the statement that followed next!

She said it as if were a very simple and ordinary thing for her. It could be to you, but not to me! I was scared of her and many ladies, therefore, in college! To me, a human life is so sacred that one should not even contemplate ending it that cheaply! That, my friend, is the true definition of greed! Do not be caught in that kind of web. You will never be happy and shall die a very painful death. Wealth that is acquired in such a manner is a curse. I may be wrong, I may also be right. You have a choice to believe me or not. I have said it to you. That is my stand!

Money making should be like a sport. You do not have to injure anyone to win. Though, it is possible that, to some, killing others is a sport. You need to enjoy and the other party also needs to have his/her fair share of the reward. And wealth is a responsibility. The more you have the more responsible you are expected to be. So be a good steward and make your money in a very clean and honorable way. You must design a true and ethical plan and work on it. It will certainly pay and you will be happy. That is why one of my business values is to always give more than I am paid for.

People will advise you differently. Others believe it is not possible to be truly successful using purely honest and above board scales. That is a lie! True wealth that brings fulfillment to the owner and to the society is acquired the Godly way. No one can talk me out of that. And I know that only evil people would reason otherwise, as well as those who will never make any reasonable amount of money because of their poor attitude about wealth.

Envy is another disaster! It has caused many people to perish without realizing their dreams. If you really understood what we talked about in the chapter about Attitude or Feelings, then you should be able to relate why envy cannot support a success mindset. Envy makes you feel bad when you see or hear about someone else's success. It makes you feel like "why him again!" sort of thing. It will cause you to talk ill about others, belittling their achievements, trying to downplay their praises. It is an evil thing and true success is that you celebrate with people when they succeed and feel happy for them; even thanking GOD for them and praying for them. Only then do you prove that you equally deserve to grow into a mountain; a mountain that cannot be hidden, that cannot go unnoticed, that is memorable and a source of blessing to others. Therefore, do not create bottlenecks for yourself. Live Your Dream! You can do it!

Chapter 7

DREAM AGAIN

At an unexpected time, after you have walked the mile and struggled, when you have paid the full price, perhaps bloody and muddy (because you cannot acquire success in credit, you must pay in full and well in advance) after you have expected and gone through all sorts of trials, you are going to meet your success smiling at you and with a warm embrace. Whatever it is that is your life's desire will come to you at a time you hardly expect it. As Napoleon Hill would say, "when it starts coming, it will come in very large portions and so fast that you will be wondering where it has been hiding all these lean years when you were desperately seeking".

It is important to know, rather, that this, almost always, comes after you have gone through the whole process; the process of conceiving a dream and moving towards it with determination that knows no meaning of quiting. After you have met all the possible disappointments and you have bravely and judiciously disappointed your disappointments with your disciplined focus and activities. After the pains of masterful labor with positive attitude and detoxifying yourself of the unproductive habits. After going that extra mile with enthusiasm again and again.

Dear friend, let me guarantee you, success will surely come and you will certainly Live Your Dream! Success leaves tracks and so we have learnt and known that there is a track to follow and meet it. We have learnt that it likes hiding and keeping at bay to test you just like an eagle tests a mate before allowing him in. As I said, success is shy, and thus will not come seeking for you. You are the one to go seek and seduce and prove to it that you are worth being its host.

Could Be Earlier

One other interesting thing in this journey is that you may actually achieve your dreams much earlier than you expected. It all depends on how your mind picked the information, about your goals. This is the reason I tell people that the language you use in setting your goals and in your day-to-day conversation is very important.

When I had expected that it would take me about 10 years or more in order to get admission into a university for my undergraduate studies, it took me a record time of just about four years. It was, to me, a miracle! Again, having finished my degree course and getting into the job market, it took less than my estimated five years to get into my own business and leave the employment world. Remember that I did not have an idea yet, when I set the five years limit, what sort of business I would be involved in. This principle has demonstrated itself to me every time and again. I know, that your success may surprise you by coming much earlier than you expected, which is a great thing, or it may still delay more than you expected. It will all depend on your predisposition to these strategies I have shared with you. Every time it delays, it has something to do with you. Take time to evaluate what mental picture enters your mind. My financial freedom is still a goal in itself and it is one of the goals that have taken a little longer. Though, I see my milestones getting achieved one after the other, an indication that I am on the right track. I have come to appreciate that we must accept blame if our lives are messed up, just as much as we accept praise whenever things go well with us. Why? Because, a man is what he thinks! And he has free-will to change the thoughts.

Excitement In The Process

Soon after celebrating your achievement, you will realize that things are getting normal again because your lifestyle has really adjusted and thus the success you have achieved stops looking really big. Do not let that snatch you the opportunity to enjoy your win and to give glory to GOD. Be grateful every step you make and cherish every moment you have because it is the attitude of gratitude that brings about more and more success and lasting joy. Also, do not let the hunger for your dreams stop you from enjoying the journey. You must enjoy every bit of the journey as that forms a great part of your life. Enjoy the difficulties and disappointments. Yes! It is possible to enjoy the difficulties when you know that it is the path to glory; a step towards your dream. It is night that gives way to daylight. It is winter that gives way to spring. Positive attitude is the central point here. Have a way to ensure you do not regret any moment. Find a reason to enjoy every second of your journey. If you left Nairobi for New York city for a business conference, and you did not take time to enjoy the journey, the spectacular moments on the way, the music, video or even slumber...then you have just wasted a part of your life. And the major reason you should enjoy these

> *In learning, you will teach. And in teaching, you will learn.*
>
> *---Phil Collins---*

things is because, therein lurks the lessons to keep you going and make you wise. It also gives you stamina and food for the journey. It forms part of the wealth of information that you shall require when advising younger people (in the success journey) who are coming after you. So, enjoy the journey and have fun. Do not abscond and slaughter the precious gift of this moment at the altar of a future dream! Live Your Dream now! It is great for your attitude.

Passing the Baton

Successful people want to help others to succeed. Otherwise you really do not deserve to succeed. There is need for more people to be very successful, rich and happy. It is common sense that when more people are successful, the society will be much better. Churches shall be built well and in record time, pupils will be better schooled, scholarship opportunities shall be more, better hospitals and more amenities shall be provided because donors are many. Better roads shall be built and quality of life shall improve. If you find yourself in a community where majority are poor and you are the only successful person, there is nothing much to celebrate because you may not help enough people as you may want. It is therefore prudent that once you have crossed your Jordan to the promised land, help others, in the best way possible, which I believe is education, to be able to cross too. Show them the way and guide them through. Become a mentor.

I do not believe in handouts and gifts without education. That leads to dependence and slavery as opposed to independence and dignity. Coach people on the ways of money, business, wisdom, lessons of history, leadership, teamwork, relationship among other important skills. You will be much happier and more secure. And you can do it! Live Your Dream!

See you at the top!

www.ingramcontent.com/pod-product-compliance
Lightning Source LLC
LaVergne TN
LVHW041154080426
835511LV00006B/587

* 9 7 8 9 9 6 6 1 0 3 1 5 4 *